This Book Belongs To
Contact Details

scan to get latest information from
Parks Canada

From all of us at **Green Peacock Wellness** and **Mountain Top Books**, we want to thank you for making the right choice of purchasing this kids' log book. Inside, you will find two pages dedicated to each national park in Canada; The first, a guided journal page, and the second, a blank page - where stamps and passports can be added, and other personalized information written/sketched.

On the first page, there are at least 8 suggested must-see attractions for each park. While care have been taken to make sure these suggestions are kids friendly as at when this book was compiled, we can't make any guarantees. We implore all readers to seek park rangers/staff advise before embarking to visit any of the parks. Better still, the QR-Code provided for each park can be used to get up-to-date information about each park.

Finally, at the end of this log book, blank pages have been included for new parks that might be established in the future. We hope kids have fun while using our book. We also welcome honest reviews, as they help us improve our service. Have fun!

Table of Contents

Table of Contents

National Park	Description	Date Visited
Akami-UapishkU-KakKasuak-Mealy Mountains	Located in the Labrador region of Newfoundland and Labrador, and established on July 31, 2015. "Akami–UapishkU" is the Innu name for the area, meaning White Mountain across, while "KakKasuak" is the Labrador Inuit word for mountain. It protects a large portion of boreal forest, tundra and more than 50 km of shoreline on the Labrador Sea and Lake Melville.	
Aulavik	Located on Banks Island in the Northwest Territories, and established in August, 1992. The name in Inuvialuktun means "place where people travel" It has the highest concentration of muskoxen on earth, with approximately 75,000 animals. It is a polar desert	
Auyuittuq	Located on Baffin Island's Cumberland Peninsula, in the Qikiqtaaluk Region of Nunavut. It was established in 1972 as a national park reserve, but redesignated a national park in 2000. The name in Inuktitut means "the land that never melts" There is little vegetation due to the cold weather, and many of the plants grow in clumps to create their own warmer "microclimate" to survive the harsh Arctic conditions	
Banff	Located in Alberta's Rocky Mountains about 150km west of Calgary. It is Canada's oldest national park, established on November 25, 1885 as Banff Hot Springs Reserve. It was established due to conflicting claims over who had the first right of claim over the discovery of the hot springs	
Bruce Peninsula	Located on the Bruce Peninsula in Ontario. It was officially established in 1987. Due to its clear water and numerous shipwrecks, scuba diving is popular in the park. It is one of the largest protected areas in southern Ontario, forming the core of UNESCO's Niagara Escarpment World Biosphere Reserve	
Cape Breton Highlands	An extension of the Appalachian mountain chain consisting of mountainous plateau across the northern part of Cape Breton Island in Nova Scotia. The interior of the plateau has no public roads and very little human presence, making it one of Nova Scotia's largest wilderness areas.	
Black Canyon of the Gunnison	Located in east Edmonton, along the Yellowhead Highway, which goes through the park. It is Canada's eighth smallest park in area size but largest fully enclosed national park, with an area of 194 km² The park was established in 1913. It is popular for being the site of the first museum ever dedicated to Ukrainian immigrants in Canada. A variety of mammal species including coyote, bison, moose, mule deer, lynx, beaver, elk, white-tailed deer, and porcupine are year-round residents.	
Forillon	Located at the outer tip of the Gaspé Peninsula of Quebec and the first national park in Quebec. The park includes forests, sea coast, salt marshes, sand dunes, cliffs, and the Eastern End of the Appalachians. On 14 February 2011, the House of Commons adopted a motion which issued an official apology to the people whose properties were expropriated to create the park.	

National Park	Description	Date Visited
Fundy	Located on the Bay of Fundy, near the village of Alma, New Brunswick, and officially opened on 29 July, 1950. It offers a rugged coastline which rises up to the Canadian Highlands, the highest tides in the world and more than 25 waterfalls.	
Georgian Bay Islands	Consists of 63 small islands or parts of islands in Georgian Bay, near Port Severn, Ontario. It was established in 1929. It is home to woodland caribou, white-tailed deer, moose, black bear, coyote, timber wolf, lynx, bobcat, porcupine, raccoon, beaver, fox, chipmunk, red squirrel, hognose snake, eastern fox snake, and the threatened eastern Massasauga rattlesnake	
Glacier	Located in the Columbia-Shuswap, British Columbia. It was established on October 10, 1886. The park preserves high peaks, large, active glaciers, and one of Canada's largest cave systems. Its dense forests support populations of large mammals, birds, and alpine species. The region is noted for its heavy snowfall.	
Grasslands	Located near the village of Val Marie, Saskatchewan and named a national park in 1981. It preserves Prairie Grasslands natural region, protecting one of the nation's few remaining areas of undisturbed dry mixed-grass/shortgrass prairie grassland.	
Gros Morne	Located on the west coast of Newfoundland. It was designated a national park on October 1, 2005. It is the second largest national park in Atlantic Canada. Being "a rare example of the process of continental drift, where deep ocean crust and the rocks of the earth's mantle lie exposed" the park was awarded the World Heritage Site status by UNESCO in 1987.	
Gulf Islands	Located on and around the Gulf Islands in British Columbia. It was established on May 9, 2003. The park is the only place in Canada with a Mediterranean climate of dry, sunny summers and mild, wet winters, the result of a rain shadow effect from surrounding mountains between the region and the ocean.	
Gwaii Haanas	Located in southernmost Haida Gwaii, 130 km off the mainland of British Columbia. The park was established in 1988. The Haida Heritage Site is within the territory of the Haida people, who have lived in Haida Gwaii for at least 14,000 years. This site is contained within the park. "Gwaii Haanas" means "Islands of Beauty" in X̱aayda kíl, the language of the Haida people	
Ivvavik	Located in Yukon. It was established in 1984, as Northern Yukon National Park. It was renamed Ivvavik in 1992 for the Inuvialuktun word meaning "nursery" or "birthplace," in reference to the importance of the area as a calving ground for caribou.	
Jasper	Located north of Banff National Park and west of Edmonton in Alberta. It is named after Jasper Hawes, who operated a trading post in the region for the North West Company. The park was established on September 14, 1907. It was declared a UNESCO World Heritage Site in 1984	

National Park	Description	Date Visited
Kejimkujik	Located within three municipalities, Annapolis, Queens and Digby of Nova Scotia peninsula. It was established in 1967. The park is named after Kejimikujik Lake, the largest lake in the park. it consists of two separate land areas: an inland part, which is coincident with the Kejimkujik National Historic Site, and the Kejimkujik National Park Seaside on the Atlantic coast.	
Kluane	Located in Yukon, it was established in 1972. Mountains, inclusive of the highest mountain in Canada, Mount Logan at 5,959 metres and glaciers dominate 83% of the park's landscape. Rafting on the Alsek River (a Canadian Heritage river), mountain biking on old mining roads, horseback riding through the Alsek Pass, boating on Kathleen Lake and Mush Lake are among activities available in the park.	
Kootenay	Located in southeastern British Columbia. Established on 21 April, 1920 as "Kootenay Dominion Park". The park's main attractions are the Radium Hot Springs, the Paint Pots, Sinclair Canyon, Marble Canyon, and Olive Lake.	
Kouchibouguac	Located on the east coast of New Brunswick, in Kouchibouguac, and established in 1969. The park includes barrier islands, sand dunes, lagoons, salt marshes and forests. It provides habitat for seabirds, including the endangered piping plover, harbor seals, grey seals, fisher marten, and the second largest tern colony in North America.	
La Mauricie	Located in Saint-Mathieu-du-Parc, Quebec. It was officially designated as a national park on 2 December, 1980. The park is named after Saint-Maurice River to the east of the park. It has more than 150 lakes of various sizes. Wildlife like moose, black bears, beavers, otters and rare wood turtle call it home. A popular location for camping, canoeing and kayaking.	
Mingan Archipelago	Located in Minganie Regional County Municipality, Quebec. It was established in 1984. It features colossal limestone outcroppings that evoke landscapes from primeval times. Frolicking whales and seals enliven the vast, blue horizon, while over 1,000 islands and islets enchant visitors with their unique flora and seabird colonies	
Mount Revelstoke	Located adjacent to the city of Revelstoke, British Columbia - the park was established in 1914. A popular skiing area and one of the first ski destinations in North America. Popular attracts include the famous Meadows-in-the-Sky Parkway, Giant Cedars Boardwalk, and Skunk Cabbage Boardwalk	
Nááts'įhch'oh	Located near the city of Tulita in Northwest Territories. It was designated a national park on December 18, 2014. The name means "stands like a porcupine" in the Dene language. The park is home to grizzly bear, Dall's sheep, mountain goats, and woodland caribou	

National Park	Description	Date Visited
Nahanni	Located in the Dehcho Region of the Northwest Territories, and established in 1972. The indigenous Dene language name for the area means "river of the land of the Nah?a people" One of the world's first four natural heritage locations to be inscribed as World Heritage Sites by UNESCO in 1978 because of its picturesque wild rivers, canyons, and waterfalls	
Pacific Rim	Located in Vancouver Island of British Columbia, and established in 1970. It comprises three separate regions: Long Beach, the Broken Group Islands, and the West Coast Trail. Long Beach is used for surfing, the Broken Group for sea kayaking, and the West Coast Trail for hiking. All regions are great for camping and scuba diving	
Point Pelee	Located in Essex County, Ontario. It was established on 29 May, 1918. The park is the southernmost part of mainland Canada. The word pelée is French for 'bald'. It is the first national park in Canada to be established for conservation. It consists of a peninsula of land, mainly of marsh and woodland habitats	
Prince Albert	Located about 200km north of Saskatoon in Saskatchewan, and established on March 24, 1927. The most visited period is from May to September. Although most people visit the park in summer, the best wildlife watching is often in the winter.	
Prince Edward Island	Located in Prince Edward Island. It was established in 1937. It protects many broad sand beaches, sand dunes, freshwater wetlands and saltmarshes. It has been designated a Canadian Important Bird Area due to the presences of nesting habitats on its beaches.	
Pukaskwa	Located south of the town of Marathon in Ontario. Established in 1978. The indigenous name of the park has debatable meaning. Thousand year old rock structures known as Pukaskwa Pits which were created by the original inhabitants can be found on many of the park's cobblestone beaches.	
Qausuittuq	Located northwest of Bathurst Island in Nunavut. It was established on September 1, 2015. The Inuktitut name means "place where the sun does not rise" It protects endangered Peary caribou and is a traditional hunting and fishing area that has sustained Inuit of Resolute Bay since the time of their relocation in the 1950's.	
Quttinirpaaq	Located in Ellesmere Island. It was established as Ellesmere Island National Park Reserve in 1988, and the name was changed to Quttinirpaaq in 1999. The name means "top of the world" in Inuktitut. The park is remarkable for its extensive glaciers, ice caps, desert-like conditions, and life forms that are uniquely adapted to extreme polar environment.	

National Park	Description	Date Visited
Riding Mountain	Located in Manitoba and established on May 30, 1933. It is located within Treaty 2 Territory. It protects three different ecosystems that converge in the area; grasslands, upland boreal and eastern deciduous forests.	
Rouge	Located in Greater Toronto, Ontario, and designated a national urban park on May 15, 2015. It protects amazing biodiversity, some of the last remaining working farms in the Greater Toronto Area, Carolinian ecosystems, Toronto's only campground, hiking trails, and human history dating back over 10,000 years.	
Sable Island	Located on Halifax, Nova Scotia. It was established on June 20, 2013. Sable Island derived its name from the French word for "sand". It lacks natural trees being covered instead with marram grass and other low-growing vegetation, and its notable for its feral horses.	
Sirmilik	Located in Qikiqtaaluk, Nunavut. It was established in 2001. In the Inuktitut "Sirmilik" means "place of glaciers". The park was first established as a bird sanctuary in 1965 and monitored by the Canadian Wildlife Service because of its seabird colonies.	
Terra Nova	Located in Sandringham, Newfoundland and Labrador. It was established in 1957. It also protects an area containing remnants of the Beothuk Nation, as well as many of the early pioneer European settlements in the region.	
Thaidene Nëné	Located in North Slave Region, Northwest Territories. It was established on 21 August, 2019. The name means "Land of the Ancestors". For the Łutsël K'é Dene First Nation, it is the heart of their homeland and a sacred place. It protects the vicinity covering the east arm of Great Slave Lake	
Thousand Islands	Located in United Counties of Leeds and Grenville, Ontario, and established in 1904. It was formerly known as the St. Lawrence Islands National Park. The park consists of 21 islands plus many smaller islets, 2 mainland properties and a visitor center.	
Torngat Mountains	Located on the Labrador Peninsula in Newfoundland and Labrador. It was established on July 10, 2008. The name comes from the Inuktitut word Tongait meaning "place of spirits". It is an Inuit homeland, a treasury of the powerful stories, spirits and traditions.	
Tuktut Nogait	Located in the Northwest Territories, and established in 1998. The name "young caribou" in Inuvialuktun. It preserves rolling hills, three major rivers, steep canyons, waterfalls, rare Bluenose west caribou and other wildlife.	
Ukkusiksalik	Located in Nunavut, and established on August 23, 2003. The name means "where there is material for the stone pot" in the local dialect. The park preserves a reversing waterfall, 500+ archeological sites and wildlife such as polar bears, grizzly bears, Arctic wolf, barren-ground caribou, seals and peregrine falcons.	

National Park	Description	Date Visited
Vuntut	Located in northern Yukon, and established in 1995. he park was established as part of the Vuntut Gwitchin First Nation Final Agreement, to conserve, protect and present to Canadians a portion of the North Yukon Natural Region which is a part of their tradition and culture.	
Wapusk	Located on the shores of Hudson Bay in the Hudson Plains ecozone of Manitoba, and established in 1996. The name comes from the Cree word for polar bear. It preserves Cape Churchill, which is known as the best location in the world to view and photograph wild polar bears.	
Waterton Lakes	Located in the southwest corner of Alberta, and established in 1895. The main tourist season is during July and August. It offers many scenic trails, a world historic site, and also serves as a biosphere reserve.	
Wood Buffalo	Located in northeastern Alberta and the southern Northwest Territories. It was established in 1922. It is the second largest national park in the world. It protects the world's largest herd of free-roaming wood bison and Alberta's largest spring by volume.	
Yoho	Located within the Rocky Mountains in southeastern British Columbia. It was established on October 10, 1886. Its name is a Cree expression for amazement or awe. It preserves popular sites like; Takakkaw Falls (the 2nd tallest waterfall in Canada), Wapta Falls, and the Burgess Shale.	

National Parks by Provinces and Territories

ALBERTA
- ④ Banff
- ⑦ Elk Island
- ⑰ Jasper
- ㊻ Waterton Lakes
- ㊼ Wood Buffalo

BRITISH COLUMBIA
- ⑪ Glacier
- ⑭ Gulf Islands
- ⑮ Gwaii Haanas
- ⑳ Kootenay
- ㉔ Mount Revelstoke
- ㉗ Pacific Rim
- ㊽ Yoho

MANITOBA
- ㉞ Riding Mountain
- ㊺ Wapusk

NEW BRUNSWICK
- ㉜ Fundy
- ㉑ Kouchibouguac

NEWFOUNDLAND & LABRADOR
- ① Akami–Uapishku – KakKasuak – Mealy Mountains
- ⑬ Gros Morne
- ㊳ Terra Nova
- ㊶ Torngat Mountains

NORTHWEST TERRITORIES
- ② Aulavik
- ㉕ Nááts'ihch'oh
- ㉖ Nahanni
- ㊴ Thaidene Nene
- ㊷ Tuktut Nogait
- ㊼ Wood Buffalo

NOVA SCOTIA
- ⑥ Cape Breton Highlands
- ⑱ Kejimkujik
- ㊱ Sable Island

NUNAVUT
- ③ Auyuittuq
- ㉜ Qausuittuq
- ㉝ Quttinirpaaq
- ㊲ Sirmilik
- ㊸ Ukkusiksalik

ONTARIO
- ⑤ Bruce Peninsula
- ⑩ Georgian Bay Islands
- ㉛ Pukaskwa
- ㉘ Point Pelee
- ㉟ Rouge
- ㊵ Thousand Islands

PRINCE EDWARD ISLAND
- ㉚ Prince Edward Island

Quebec
- ⑧ Forillon
- ㉒ La Mauricie
- ㉓ Mingan Archipelago

SASKATCHEWAN
- ⑫ Grasslands
- ㉙ Prince Albert

Yukon
- ⑯ Ivvavik
- ⑲ Kluane
- ㊹ Vuntut

vii

Map Showing National Parks Location

Essential Gear

- [ ] This Book!
- [ ] Park Map
- [ ] Camera
- [ ] Sweater
- [ ] Binoculars
- [ ] Magnifying Glass
- [ ] Insect Repellent
- [ ] Water Bottle
- [ ] Snacks
- [ ] Swimsuit
- [ ] Towel
- [ ] First Aid Kit
- [ ] Hat
- [ ] Sunblock
- [ ] Pen/pencil
- [ ] Backpack
- [ ] Field Guide
- [ ] Trash Bag
- [ ] ----------
- [ ] ----------
- [ ] ----------
- [ ] ----------
- [ ] ----------
- [ ] ----------
- [ ] ----------

- [ ] ----------
- [ ] ----------
- [ ] ----------
- [ ] ----------
- [ ] ----------
- [ ] ----------
- [ ] ----------
- [ ] ----------
- [ ] ----------
- [ ] ----------
- [ ] ----------
- [ ] ----------
- [ ] ----------
- [ ] ----------
- [ ] ----------
- [ ] ----------
- [ ] ----------
- [ ] ----------
- [ ] ----------
- [ ] ----------
- [ ] ----------
- [ ] ----------
- [ ] ----------
- [ ] ----------
- [ ] ----------

- [ ] ----------
- [ ] ----------
- [ ] ----------
- [ ] ----------
- [ ] ----------
- [ ] ----------
- [ ] ----------
- [ ] ----------
- [ ] ----------
- [ ] ----------
- [ ] ----------
- [ ] ----------
- [ ] ----------
- [ ] ----------
- [ ] ----------
- [ ] ----------
- [ ] ----------
- [ ] ----------
- [ ] ----------
- [ ] ----------
- [ ] ----------
- [ ] ----------
- [ ] ----------
- [ ] ----------
- [ ] ----------

Akami-Uapishkᵁ-KakKasuak-Mealy Mountains

Newfoundland and Labrador | Est.: 2015 | Area (km²): 10,700 | Coord.: 53° 24′ 00″ N, 59° 22′ 00″ W

Date: Temp.:   Who I went with:

Weather: ☀ ⛅ ☁ ❄ 🌦 💨
⬜ ⬜ ⬜ ⬜ ⬜ ⬜   Lodging:

Season:

⬜ Spring ⬜ Summer ⬜ Fall ⬜ Winter   Fee(s):   ⬜ Free:

Favorite moment:

Sights:

Wildlife:

Popular attractions:

⬜ The Wunderstrand   ⬜ ....
⬜ The Aurora Borealis   ⬜ ....
⬜ Cave Creature Lake   ⬜ ....
⬜ Mealy Mountains   ⬜ ....
⬜ Lake Melville   ⬜ ....
⬜ Awesome Lake   ⬜ ....
⬜ Sandwich Bay   ⬜ ....

of day(s) of visit

⬜ 1 ⬜ 2 ⬜ 3 ⬜ 3+

Overall Experience

10

Journal, Sketch, Photo & Passport Page

PHOTO & STAMP HERE

Essential Gear

- ☐ This Book!
- ☐ Park Map
- ☐ Camera
- ☐ Sweater
- ☐ Binoculars
- ☐ Magnifying Glass
- ☐ Insect Repellent
- ☐ Water Bottle
- ☐ Snacks
- ☐ Swimsuit
- ☐ Towel
- ☐ First Aid Kit
- ☐ Hat
- ☐ Sunblock
- ☐ Pen/pencil
- ☐ Backpack
- ☐ Field Guide
- ☐ Trash Bag
- ☐ -----------
- ☐ -----------
- ☐ -----------
- ☐ -----------
- ☐ -----------
- ☐ -----------
- ☐ -----------

- ☐ -----------
- ☐ -----------
- ☐ -----------
- ☐ -----------
- ☐ -----------
- ☐ -----------
- ☐ -----------
- ☐ -----------
- ☐ -----------
- ☐ -----------
- ☐ -----------
- ☐ -----------
- ☐ -----------
- ☐ -----------
- ☐ -----------
- ☐ -----------
- ☐ -----------
- ☐ -----------
- ☐ -----------
- ☐ -----------
- ☐ -----------
- ☐ -----------
- ☐ -----------
- ☐ -----------
- ☐ -----------

- ☐ -----------
- ☐ -----------
- ☐ -----------
- ☐ -----------
- ☐ -----------
- ☐ -----------
- ☐ -----------
- ☐ -----------
- ☐ -----------
- ☐ -----------
- ☐ -----------
- ☐ -----------
- ☐ -----------
- ☐ -----------
- ☐ -----------
- ☐ -----------
- ☐ -----------
- ☐ -----------
- ☐ -----------
- ☐ -----------
- ☐ -----------
- ☐ -----------
- ☐ -----------
- ☐ -----------
- ☐ -----------

Aulavik

Northwest Territories | Est.: 1992 | Area (km²): 12,200 | Coord.: 73° 42′ 01″ N, 119° 55′ 10″ W

Date: Temp.:

Who I went with:

Weather: ☀ ⛅ ☁ ❄ 🌧 💨
⬜ ⬜ ⬜ ⬜ ⬜ ⬜

Lodging:

Season:

⬜ Spring ⬜ Summer ⬜ Fall ⬜ Winter

Fee(s):   ⬜ Free:

Favorite moment:

Sights:

Wildlife:

Popular attractions:

⬜ Thomsen River
⬜ Mercy Bay
⬜ Castel Bay
⬜ Nangmagvik Lake
⬜ Sachs Harbour
⬜ Polar Bear Cabin
⬜ Shoran Lake

⬜ Nasogaluak Archaeological Site
⬜ Baker Hill Archaeological Site
⬜ Head Hill Archaeological Site
⬜ Migratory Bird Sanctuary No. 2
⬜ HMS Investigator Site
⬜ Mercy River Falls
⬜ ....

# of day(s) of visit

⬜1 ⬜2 ⬜3 ⬜3+

Overall Experience

10

Journal, Sketch, Photo & Passport Page

PHOTO & STAMP HERE

Essential Gear

- [ ] This Book!
- [ ] Park Map
- [ ] Camera
- [ ] Sweater
- [ ] Binoculars
- [ ] Magnifying Glass
- [ ] Insect Repellent
- [ ] Water Bottle
- [ ] Snacks
- [ ] Swimsuit
- [ ] Towel
- [ ] First Aid Kit
- [ ] Hat
- [ ] Sunblock
- [ ] Pen/pencil
- [ ] Backpack
- [ ] Field Guide
- [ ] Trash Bag
- [ ] ------------
- [ ] ------------
- [ ] ------------
- [ ] ------------
- [ ] ------------
- [ ] ------------
- [ ] ------------

Auyuittuq

Nunavut | Est.: 1972 | Area (km²): 21,470 | Coord.: 67° 30′ 0″ N, 66° 0′ 0″ W

Date: Temp.:   Who I went with:

Weather: ☀️ ⛅ ☁️ ❄️ 🌧️ 💨
☐ ☐ ☐ ☐ ☐ ☐   Lodging:

Season:

☐ Spring ☐ Summer ☐ Fall ☐ Winter   Fee(s):   ☐ Free:

Favorite moment:

Sights:

Wildlife:

Popular attractions:

☐ Akshayuk Pass
☐ Coronation Fjord
☐ Narpaing-Maktak Valley
☐ Mount Overlord
☐ Qikiqtarjuaq Hamlet
☐ Mount Thor
☐ Schwartzenbach Falls

☐ Owl River Valley
☐ Maktak Fiords
☐ The Penny Ice Cap
☐ Greenshield Lake
☐ Angmarlik Interpretive Centre
☐ Ukuma Trail
☐ Summit Lake

of day(s) of visit

○ 1 ○ 2 ○ 3 ○ 3+

Overall Experience

___
10

Journal, Sketch, Photo & Passport Page

PHOTO & STAMP
HERE

Essential Gear

- ☐ This Book!
- ☐ Park Map
- ☐ Camera
- ☐ Sweater
- ☐ Binoculars
- ☐ Magnifying Glass
- ☐ Insect Repellent
- ☐ Water Bottle
- ☐ Snacks
- ☐ Swimsuit
- ☐ Towel
- ☐ First Aid Kit
- ☐ Hat
- ☐ Sunblock
- ☐ Pen/pencil
- ☐ Backpack
- ☐ Field Guide
- ☐ Trash Bag
- ☐ -----------
- ☐ -----------
- ☐ -----------
- ☐ -----------
- ☐ -----------
- ☐ -----------
- ☐ -----------

- ☐ -----------
- ☐ -----------
- ☐ -----------
- ☐ -----------
- ☐ -----------
- ☐ -----------
- ☐ -----------
- ☐ -----------
- ☐ -----------
- ☐ -----------
- ☐ -----------
- ☐ -----------
- ☐ -----------
- ☐ -----------
- ☐ -----------
- ☐ -----------
- ☐ -----------
- ☐ -----------
- ☐ -----------
- ☐ -----------
- ☐ -----------
- ☐ -----------
- ☐ -----------
- ☐ -----------
- ☐ -----------

- ☐ -----------
- ☐ -----------
- ☐ -----------
- ☐ -----------
- ☐ -----------
- ☐ -----------
- ☐ -----------
- ☐ -----------
- ☐ -----------
- ☐ -----------
- ☐ -----------
- ☐ -----------
- ☐ -----------
- ☐ -----------
- ☐ -----------
- ☐ -----------
- ☐ -----------
- ☐ -----------
- ☐ -----------
- ☐ -----------
- ☐ -----------
- ☐ -----------
- ☐ -----------
- ☐ -----------
- ☐ -----------

Banff

Alberta | Est.: 1885 | Area (km²): 6641 | Coord.: 51° 36′ 0″ N, 116° 3′ 0″ W

Date: Temp.:

Who I went with:

Weather: ☀️ ⛅ ☁️ ❄️ 🌧️ 💨
☐ ☐ ☐ ☐ ☐ ☐

Lodging:

Season:

☐ Spring ☐ Summer ☐ Fall ☐ Winter

Fee(s):   ☐ Free:

Favorite moment:

Sights:

Wildlife:

Popular attractions:

☐ Upper Hot Springs
☐ Johnston Canyon
☐ National Historic Site
☐ Lake Louise
☐ Château Lake Louise
☐ Lake Louise Ski Resort
☐ Moraine Lake

☐ Lake Minnewanka
☐ Marsh Trail
☐ Banff Legacy Bike/Hike Trail
☐ Sundance Canyon Trail
☐ Icefields Parkway
☐ Bankhead Ghost Town
☐ Glacier Skywalk

# of day(s) of visit

○ 1 ○ 2 ○ 3 ○ 3+

Overall Experience

——
10

Journal, Sketch, Photo & Passport Page

PHOTO & STAMP HERE

Essential Gear

- [ ] This Book!
- [ ] Park Map
- [ ] Camera
- [ ] Sweater
- [ ] Binoculars
- [ ] Magnifying Glass
- [ ] Insect Repellent
- [ ] Water Bottle
- [ ] Snacks
- [ ] Swimsuit
- [ ] Towel
- [ ] First Aid Kit
- [ ] Hat
- [ ] Sunblock
- [ ] Pen/pencil
- [ ] Backpack
- [ ] Field Guide
- [ ] Trash Bag
- [ ] _____
- [ ] _____
- [ ] _____
- [ ] _____
- [ ] _____
- [ ] _____
- [ ] _____

- [ ] _____
- [ ] _____
- [ ] _____
- [ ] _____
- [ ] _____
- [ ] _____
- [ ] _____
- [ ] _____
- [ ] _____
- [ ] _____
- [ ] _____
- [ ] _____
- [ ] _____
- [ ] _____
- [ ] _____
- [ ] _____
- [ ] _____
- [ ] _____
- [ ] _____
- [ ] _____
- [ ] _____
- [ ] _____
- [ ] _____
- [ ] _____
- [ ] _____

- [ ] _____
- [ ] _____
- [ ] _____
- [ ] _____
- [ ] _____
- [ ] _____
- [ ] _____
- [ ] _____
- [ ] _____
- [ ] _____
- [ ] _____
- [ ] _____
- [ ] _____
- [ ] _____
- [ ] _____
- [ ] _____
- [ ] _____
- [ ] _____
- [ ] _____
- [ ] _____
- [ ] _____
- [ ] _____
- [ ] _____
- [ ] _____
- [ ] _____

Bruce Peninsula

Ontario | Est.: 1987 | Area (km²): 154 | Coord.: 45° 14' 0" N, 81° 36' 0" W

Date: Temp.:

Weather: ☀ ⛅ ☁ ❄ 🌧 💨
⬭ ⬭ ⬭ ⬭ ⬭ ⬭

Who I went with:

Lodging:

Season:

⬭ Spring   ⬭ Summer   ⬭ Fall   ⬭ Winter

Fee(s):   ⬭ Free:

Favorite moment:

Sights:

Wildlife:

Popular attractions:

⬭ Cyprus Lake Trail   ⬭ Indian Head Cove
⬭ The Grotto   ⬭ Driftwood Cove
⬭ Cyprus Lake Campground   ⬭ Horse Lake Trail
⬭ Halfway Log Dump   ⬭ Overhanging Point
⬭ Singing Sands Beach   ⬭ Marr Lake Trail
⬭ Bruce Trail   ⬭ Little Dunks Lookout
⬭ Little Cove Beach   ⬭ The Wild Garden Trail

# of day(s) of visit

◯1 ◯2 ◯3 ◯3+

Overall Experience

10

14

Journal, Sketch, Photo & Passport Page

PHOTO & STAMP HERE

_____

_____

_____

_____

_____

_____

_____

_____

_____

_____

_____

Essential Gear

- [ ] This Book!
- [ ] Park Map
- [ ] Camera
- [ ] Sweater
- [ ] Binoculars
- [ ] Magnifying Glass
- [ ] Insect Repellent
- [ ] Water Bottle
- [ ] Snacks
- [ ] Swimsuit
- [ ] Towel
- [ ] First Aid Kit
- [ ] Hat
- [ ] Sunblock
- [ ] Pen/pencil
- [ ] Backpack
- [ ] Field Guide
- [ ] Trash Bag
- [ ] _____
- [ ] _____
- [ ] _____
- [ ] _____
- [ ] _____
- [ ] _____
- [ ] _____

Cape Breton Highlands

Nova Scotia | Est.: 1936 | Area (km²): 948 | Coord.: 46° 44′ 30″ N, 60° 38′ 30″ W

Date: Temp.:

Who I went with:

Weather: ☀ ⛅ 🌧 ❄ ⛈ 🌬
◯ ◯ ◯ ◯ ◯ ◯

Lodging:

Season:

◯ Spring ◯ Summer ◯ Fall ◯ Winter

Fee(s):   ◯ Free:

Favorite moment:

Sights:

Wildlife:

Popular attractions:

◯ Cabot Trail
◯ Skyline Trail
◯ Beulach Ban Falls
◯ Mary Ann Falls
◯ Clyburn Valley
◯ Broad Cove Mountain
◯ Acadian Trail

◯ Le vieux chemin du Cap-Rouge
◯ The Lone Sheiling Heritage Site
◯ Ingonish Beach Campground
◯ MacKenzie Mountain Look-Off
◯ Lakie's Head
◯ Chéticamp Campground
◯ Sweet Discovery Story

# of day(s) of visit

◯ 1 ◯ 2 ◯ 3 ◯ 3+

Overall Experience

——
10

Journal, Sketch, Photo & Passport Page

Essential Gear

- [ ] This Book!
- [ ] Park Map
- [ ] Camera
- [ ] Sweater
- [ ] Binoculars
- [ ] Magnifying Glass
- [ ] Insect Repellent
- [ ] Water Bottle
- [ ] Snacks
- [ ] Swimsuit
- [ ] Towel
- [ ] First Aid Kit
- [ ] Hat
- [ ] Sunblock
- [ ] Pen/pencil
- [ ] Backpack
- [ ] Field Guide
- [ ] Trash Bag
- [ ] _____
- [ ] _____
- [ ] _____
- [ ] _____
- [ ] _____
- [ ] _____
- [ ] _____

- [ ] _____
- [ ] _____
- [ ] _____
- [ ] _____
- [ ] _____
- [ ] _____
- [ ] _____
- [ ] _____
- [ ] _____
- [ ] _____
- [ ] _____
- [ ] _____
- [ ] _____
- [ ] _____
- [ ] _____
- [ ] _____
- [ ] _____
- [ ] _____
- [ ] _____
- [ ] _____
- [ ] _____
- [ ] _____
- [ ] _____
- [ ] _____
- [ ] _____

- [ ] _____
- [ ] _____
- [ ] _____
- [ ] _____
- [ ] _____
- [ ] _____
- [ ] _____
- [ ] _____
- [ ] _____
- [ ] _____
- [ ] _____
- [ ] _____
- [ ] _____
- [ ] _____
- [ ] _____
- [ ] _____
- [ ] _____
- [ ] _____
- [ ] _____
- [ ] _____
- [ ] _____
- [ ] _____
- [ ] _____
- [ ] _____
- [ ] _____

Elk Island

Alberta | Est.: 1913 | Area (km²): 194 | Coord.: 53° 36′ 52″ N, 112° 51′ 58″ W

Date: Temp.:   Who I went with:

Weather: ☀ ⛅ 🌧 ❄ 🌦 🌬
         ◯ ◯ ◯ ◯ ◯ ◯   Lodging:

Season:

◯ Spring ◯ Summer ◯ Fall ◯ Winter   Fee(s):   ◯ Free:

Favorite moment:

Sights:

Wildlife:

Popular attractions: # of day(s) of visit

◯ Wood Bison Trail   ◯ The Backstage Bison Tour   ◯1 ◯2 ◯3 ◯3+

◯ Elk Island Parkway   ◯ Beaver Hills Dark Sky Preserve

◯ Astotin Lake   ◯ Bison Loop Road   **Overall**

◯ Elk Island Geocaches   ◯ Tawayik Lake Trail   **Experience**

◯ Astotin Theatre   ◯ Amisk Wuche Trail

◯ Living Waters Boardwalk ◯ Beaver Pond Trail

◯ Lakeshore Trail   ◯ Bison Backstage Tour   **10**

Journal, Sketch, Photo & Passport Page

PHOTO & STAMP HERE

Essential Gear

- ☐ This Book!
- ☐ Park Map
- ☐ Camera
- ☐ Sweater
- ☐ Binoculars
- ☐ Magnifying Glass
- ☐ Insect Repellent
- ☐ Water Bottle
- ☐ Snacks
- ☐ Swimsuit
- ☐ Towel
- ☐ First Aid Kit
- ☐ Hat
- ☐ Sunblock
- ☐ Pen/pencil
- ☐ Backpack
- ☐ Field Guide
- ☐ Trash Bag
- ☐ ----------
- ☐ ----------
- ☐ ----------
- ☐ ----------
- ☐ ----------
- ☐ ----------
- ☐ ----------

Forillon

Quebec | Est.: 1970 | Area (km²): 244 | Coord.: 48° 54′ 0″ N, 64° 21′ 0″ W

Date: Temp.:   Who I went with:

Weather: ☀ ⛅ ☁ ❄ 🌧 💨
⬭ ⬭ ⬭ ⬭ ⬭ ⬭   Lodging:

Season:

⬭ Spring ⬭ Summer ⬭ Fall ⬭ Winter   Fee(s):   ⬭ Free:

Favorite moment:

Sights:

Wildlife:

Popular attractions:

⬭ La Chute Trail   ⬭ Les Parages Trail
⬭ Mont-Saint-Alban Trail   ⬭ Hyman & Sons General Store
⬭ Blanchette Homestead   ⬭ Fort Peninsula
⬭ Dolbel-Roberts House   ⬭ Petit-Gaspé Campground
⬭ Grande-Grave Wharf   ⬭ Des-Rosiers Campground
⬭ Cape Gaspé Lighthouse   ⬭ Whale Watching Cruise
⬭ Penouille Trail   ⬭ Kite Surfing

# of day(s) of visit

○1 ○2 ○3 ○3+

Overall Experience

―――
10

Journal, Sketch, Photo & Passport Page

PHOTO & STAMP HERE

Essential Gear

- ☐ This Book!
- ☐ Park Map
- ☐ Camera
- ☐ Sweater
- ☐ Binoculars
- ☐ Magnifying Glass
- ☐ Insect Repellent
- ☐ Water Bottle
- ☐ Snacks
- ☐ Swimsuit
- ☐ Towel
- ☐ First Aid Kit
- ☐ Hat
- ☐ Sunblock
- ☐ Pen/pencil
- ☐ Backpack
- ☐ Field Guide
- ☐ Trash Bag
- ☐ ----------
- ☐ ----------
- ☐ ----------
- ☐ ----------
- ☐ ----------
- ☐ ----------
- ☐ ----------

- ☐ ----------
- ☐ ----------
- ☐ ----------
- ☐ ----------
- ☐ ----------
- ☐ ----------
- ☐ ----------
- ☐ ----------
- ☐ ----------
- ☐ ----------
- ☐ ----------
- ☐ ----------
- ☐ ----------
- ☐ ----------
- ☐ ----------
- ☐ ----------
- ☐ ----------
- ☐ ----------
- ☐ ----------
- ☐ ----------
- ☐ ----------
- ☐ ----------
- ☐ ----------
- ☐ ----------
- ☐ ----------

- ☐ ----------
- ☐ ----------
- ☐ ----------
- ☐ ----------
- ☐ ----------
- ☐ ----------
- ☐ ----------
- ☐ ----------
- ☐ ----------
- ☐ ----------
- ☐ ----------
- ☐ ----------
- ☐ ----------
- ☐ ----------
- ☐ ----------
- ☐ ----------
- ☐ ----------
- ☐ ----------
- ☐ ----------
- ☐ ----------
- ☐ ----------
- ☐ ----------
- ☐ ----------
- ☐ ----------
- ☐ ----------

Fundy

New Brunswick | Est.: 1948 | Area (km²): 207 | Coord.: 45° 37′ 0″ N, 65° 2′ 0″ W

Date: Temp.:   Who I went with:

Weather: ☀ ⛅ 🌧 ❄ 🌦 🌬
⬜ ⬜ ⬜ ⬜ ⬜ ⬜   Lodging:

Season:

⬜ Spring ⬜ Summer ⬜ Fall ⬜ Winter   Fee(s):   ⬜ Free:

Favorite moment:

Sights:

Wildlife:

Popular attractions: # of day(s) of visit

⬜ Dickson Falls   ⬜ Butland Lookout Point   ⬜1 ⬜2 ⬜3 ⬜3+

⬜ Third Vault Falls   ⬜ Milky Way Madness Tour

⬜ Laverty Falls   ⬜ The Low Tide Mudflats   **Overall**

⬜ Point Wolfe Campground ⬜ Coastal Trail   **Experience**

⬜ Molly Kool Kitchen Party ⬜ Geocaching

⬜ Black Horse Trail   ⬜ Swim With Salmons Program

⬜ The Golf Course   ⬜ Coppermine Trail   **10**

Journal, Sketch, Photo & Passport Page

PHOTO & STAMP HERE

Essential Gear

- [ ] This Book!
- [ ] Park Map
- [ ] Camera
- [ ] Sweater
- [ ] Binoculars
- [ ] Magnifying Glass
- [ ] Insect Repellent
- [ ] Water Bottle
- [ ] Snacks
- [ ] Swimsuit
- [ ] Towel
- [ ] First Aid Kit
- [ ] Hat
- [ ] Sunblock
- [ ] Pen/pencil
- [ ] Backpack
- [ ] Field Guide
- [ ] Trash Bag
- [ ] _____
- [ ] _____
- [ ] _____
- [ ] _____
- [ ] _____
- [ ] _____
- [ ] _____

Georgian Bay Islands

Ontario | Est.: 1929 | Area (km²): 13.5 | Coord.: 44° 53′ 0″ N, 79° 52′ 0″ W

Date: Temp.:

Who I went with:

Weather: ☀ ⛅ ☁ ❄ 🌧 💨
☐ ☐ ☐ ☐ ☐ ☐

Lodging:

Season:

☐ Spring ☐ Summer ☐ Fall ☐ Winter

Fee(s):   ☐ Free:

Favorite moment:

Sights:

Wildlife:

Popular attractions:

☐ Cambrian Trail
☐ Fairy Lake
☐ Huron Bike/Hike Trail
☐ Christian Bike/Hike Trail
☐ Geocaching
☐ Heritage Loop
☐ Wana Keta Picnic Area

☐ Cedar Spring Campground
☐ Christian Beach Rustic Cabins
☐ Treasure Bay Trek
☐ Honeymoon Bay
☐ Beausoleil Island Historic Site
☐ ....
☐ ....

# of day(s) of visit

○1 ○2 ○3 ○3+

Overall Experience

——
10

Journal, Sketch, Photo & Passport Page

PHOTO & STAMP HERE

Essential Gear

- [ ] This Book!
- [ ] Park Map
- [ ] Camera
- [ ] Sweater
- [ ] Binoculars
- [ ] Magnifying Glass
- [ ] Insect Repellent
- [ ] Water Bottle
- [ ] Snacks
- [ ] Swimsuit
- [ ] Towel
- [ ] First Aid Kit
- [ ] Hat
- [ ] Sunblock
- [ ] Pen/pencil
- [ ] Backpack
- [ ] Field Guide
- [ ] Trash Bag
- [ ] ----------
- [ ] ----------
- [ ] ----------
- [ ] ----------
- [ ] ----------
- [ ] ----------
- [ ] ----------

- [ ] ----------
- [ ] ----------
- [ ] ----------
- [ ] ----------
- [ ] ----------
- [ ] ----------
- [ ] ----------
- [ ] ----------
- [ ] ----------
- [ ] ----------
- [ ] ----------
- [ ] ----------
- [ ] ----------
- [ ] ----------
- [ ] ----------
- [ ] ----------
- [ ] ----------
- [ ] ----------
- [ ] ----------
- [ ] ----------
- [ ] ----------
- [ ] ----------
- [ ] ----------
- [ ] ----------
- [ ] ----------

- [ ] ----------
- [ ] ----------
- [ ] ----------
- [ ] ----------
- [ ] ----------
- [ ] ----------
- [ ] ----------
- [ ] ----------
- [ ] ----------
- [ ] ----------
- [ ] ----------
- [ ] ----------
- [ ] ----------
- [ ] ----------
- [ ] ----------
- [ ] ----------
- [ ] ----------
- [ ] ----------
- [ ] ----------
- [ ] ----------
- [ ] ----------
- [ ] ----------
- [ ] ----------
- [ ] ----------
- [ ] ----------

Glacier

Montana | Est.: 1910 | Area (km²): 4,102 | Coord.: 51° 16′ 0″ N, 117° 31′ 0″ W

Date: Temp.:   Who I went with:

Weather: ☀ ⛅ 🌧 ❄ 🌦 💨
⬭ ⬭ ⬭ ⬭ ⬭ ⬭   Lodging:

Season:

⬭ Spring ⬭ Summer ⬭ Fall ⬭ Winter   Fee(s):   ⬭ Free:

Favorite moment:

Sights:

Wildlife:

Popular attractions:

- ⬭ Rock Garden Trail
- ⬭ Glacier Crest Trail
- ⬭ The Meeting of the Waters
- ⬭ Asulkan Valley
- ⬭ Avalanche Crest
- ⬭ Beaver River Valley
- ⬭ Bear Creek Falls

- ⬭ Rogers Pass Discovery Centre
- ⬭ Roger's Pass Summit
- ⬭ Mount Sir Donald Picnic Area
- ⬭ Roger Pass Ski
- ⬭ Hemlock Grove Boardwalk
- ⬭ Forest And Fire Nature Trail
- ⬭ 1885 Rails Trail

# of day(s) of visit

◯1 ◯2 ◯3 ◯3+

Overall Experience

⎯⎯
10

Journal, Sketch, Photo & Passport Page

PHOTO & STAMP
HERE

Essential Gear

- [ ] This Book!
- [ ] Park Map
- [ ] Camera
- [ ] Sweater
- [ ] Binoculars
- [ ] Magnifying Glass
- [ ] Insect Repellent
- [ ] Water Bottle
- [ ] Snacks
- [ ] Swimsuit
- [ ] Towel
- [ ] First Aid Kit
- [ ] Hat
- [ ] Sunblock
- [ ] Pen/pencil
- [ ] Backpack
- [ ] Field Guide
- [ ] Trash Bag
- [ ] ----------
- [ ] ----------
- [ ] ----------
- [ ] ----------
- [ ] ----------
- [ ] ----------
- [ ] ----------

- [ ] ----------
- [ ] ----------
- [ ] ----------
- [ ] ----------
- [ ] ----------
- [ ] ----------
- [ ] ----------
- [ ] ----------
- [ ] ----------
- [ ] ----------
- [ ] ----------
- [ ] ----------
- [ ] ----------
- [ ] ----------
- [ ] ----------
- [ ] ----------
- [ ] ----------
- [ ] ----------
- [ ] ----------
- [ ] ----------
- [ ] ----------
- [ ] ----------
- [ ] ----------
- [ ] ----------
- [ ] ----------

- [ ] ----------
- [ ] ----------
- [ ] ----------
- [ ] ----------
- [ ] ----------
- [ ] ----------
- [ ] ----------
- [ ] ----------
- [ ] ----------
- [ ] ----------
- [ ] ----------
- [ ] ----------
- [ ] ----------
- [ ] ----------
- [ ] ----------
- [ ] ----------
- [ ] ----------
- [ ] ----------
- [ ] ----------
- [ ] ----------
- [ ] ----------
- [ ] ----------
- [ ] ----------
- [ ] ----------
- [ ] ----------

Grasslands

Saskatchewan | Est.: 1981 | Area (km²): 907 | Coord.: 49° 5′ 27″ N, 107° 9′ 50″ W

Date: Temp.: | Who I went with:

Weather: ☼ ⛅ ☁ ❄ 🌧 💨
⬭ ⬭ ⬭ ⬭ ⬭ ⬭ | Lodging:

Season:

⬭ Spring ⬭ Summer ⬭ Fall ⬭ Winter | Fee(s):   ⬭ Free:

Favorite moment:

Sights:

Wildlife:

Popular attractions:

⬭ Valley of 1,000 Devils   ⬭ 70 Mile Butte Trail
⬭ Rock Creek Trail   ⬭ Rim Walk Trail
⬭ Badlands Parkway   ⬭ The Ecotour Scenic Drive
⬭ Rock Creek Campground   ⬭ Zahurski Point Route
⬭ The Frenchman River   ⬭ Equestrian Camping
⬭ Eagle Butte Trail   ⬭ Otter Basin
⬭ Three Sisters Trail   ⬭ Geocaching

of day(s) of visit

◯1 ◯2 ◯3 ◯3+

Overall Experience

10

Journal, Sketch, Photo & Passport Page

PHOTO & STAMP HERE

Essential Gear

- ☐ This Book!
- ☐ Park Map
- ☐ Camera
- ☐ Sweater
- ☐ Binoculars
- ☐ Magnifying Glass
- ☐ Insect Repellent
- ☐ Water Bottle
- ☐ Snacks
- ☐ Swimsuit
- ☐ Towel
- ☐ First Aid Kit
- ☐ Hat
- ☐ Sunblock
- ☐ Pen/pencil
- ☐ Backpack
- ☐ Field Guide
- ☐ Trash Bag
- ☐ ------------
- ☐ ------------
- ☐ ------------
- ☐ ------------
- ☐ ------------
- ☐ ------------
- ☐ ------------

Gros Morne

Newfoundland and Labrador | Est.: 2005 | Area (km²): 1,805 | Coord.: 49° 41′ 22″ N, 57° 44′ 17″ W

Date:　　　Temp.:

Weather: ☀ ⛅ ☁ ❄ 🌧 💨
◯ ◯ ◯ ◯ ◯ ◯

Season:

◯ Spring　◯ Summer　◯ Fall　◯ Winter

Who I went with:

Lodging:

Fee(s):　　　　　　　　◯ Free:

Favorite moment:

Sights:

Wildlife:

Popular attractions:

◯ The Tablelands　　　　◯ Lobster Cove Head Lighthouse

◯ Western Brook Pond　　◯ Baker's Brook Falls

◯ Gros Morne Mountain　◯ Green Gardens Trail

◯ Stuckless Pond Trail　　◯ The Discovery Centre

◯ Lookout Hills Trail　　　◯ Green Point Geological Site

◯ The Geocaching Challenge　◯ Woody Point Heritage Walk

◯ Burridges Gulch Ski Area　◯ Berry Hill Campground

of day(s) of visit

◯1 ◯2 ◯3 ◯3+

Overall Experience

10

Journal, Sketch, Photo & Passport Page

PHOTO & STAMP HERE

Essential Gear

- ☐ This Book!
- ☐ Park Map
- ☐ Camera
- ☐ Sweater
- ☐ Binoculars
- ☐ Magnifying Glass
- ☐ Insect Repellent
- ☐ Water Bottle
- ☐ Snacks
- ☐ Swimsuit
- ☐ Towel
- ☐ First Aid Kit
- ☐ Hat
- ☐ Sunblock
- ☐ Pen/pencil
- ☐ Backpack
- ☐ Field Guide
- ☐ Trash Bag
- ☐ ----------
- ☐ ----------
- ☐ ----------
- ☐ ----------
- ☐ ----------
- ☐ ----------
- ☐ ----------

Gulf Islands

British Columbia | Est.: 2003 | Area (km²): 36 | Coord.: 48° 47′ 0″ N, 123° 18′ 0″ W

Date: Temp.:   Who I went with:

Weather: ☀ ⛅ 🌧 ❄ ⛈ 🌬
⬜ ⬜ ⬜ ⬜ ⬜ ⬜   Lodging:

Season:

⬜ Spring ⬜ Summer ⬜ Fall ⬜ Winter   Fee(s):   ⬜ Free:

Favorite moment:

Sights:

Wildlife:

Popular attractions:

⬜ Roesland Orchard   ⬜ Georgina Point
⬜ James Bay Orchard   ⬜ Winter Cove
⬜ Whale Watching   ⬜ Arbutus Point Campground
⬜ Mount Warburton Peak   ⬜ Lyall Creek
⬜ Maria Mahoi Homestead   ⬜ Cabbage Island
⬜ The Geocaching Challenge ⬜ ....
⬜ Mount Norman Viewpoint ⬜ ....

# of day(s) of visit

◯ 1 ◯ 2 ◯ 3 ◯ 3+

Overall Experience

10

Journal, Sketch, Photo & Passport Page

PHOTO & STAMP HERE

Essential Gear

- ☐ This Book!
- ☐ Park Map
- ☐ Camera
- ☐ Sweater
- ☐ Binoculars
- ☐ Magnifying Glass
- ☐ Insect Repellent
- ☐ Water Bottle
- ☐ Snacks
- ☐ Swimsuit
- ☐ Towel
- ☐ First Aid Kit
- ☐ Hat
- ☐ Sunblock
- ☐ Pen/pencil
- ☐ Backpack
- ☐ Field Guide
- ☐ Trash Bag
- ☐ ----------
- ☐ ----------
- ☐ ----------
- ☐ ----------
- ☐ ----------
- ☐ ----------
- ☐ ----------

- ☐ ----------
- ☐ ----------
- ☐ ----------
- ☐ ----------
- ☐ ----------
- ☐ ----------
- ☐ ----------
- ☐ ----------
- ☐ ----------
- ☐ ----------
- ☐ ----------
- ☐ ----------
- ☐ ----------
- ☐ ----------
- ☐ ----------
- ☐ ----------
- ☐ ----------
- ☐ ----------
- ☐ ----------
- ☐ ----------
- ☐ ----------
- ☐ ----------
- ☐ ----------
- ☐ ----------
- ☐ ----------

- ☐ ----------
- ☐ ----------
- ☐ ----------
- ☐ ----------
- ☐ ----------
- ☐ ----------
- ☐ ----------
- ☐ ----------
- ☐ ----------
- ☐ ----------
- ☐ ----------
- ☐ ----------
- ☐ ----------
- ☐ ----------
- ☐ ----------
- ☐ ----------
- ☐ ----------
- ☐ ----------
- ☐ ----------
- ☐ ----------
- ☐ ----------
- ☐ ----------
- ☐ ----------
- ☐ ----------
- ☐ ----------

Gwaii Haanas

British Columbia | Est.: 1988 | Area (km²): 1,470 | Coord.: 52° 21′ 0″ N, 131° 26′ 0″ W

Date: Temp.:   Who I went with:

Weather: ☀ ⛅ ☁ ❄ 🌧 💨
         ☐ ☐ ☐ ☐ ☐ ☐   Lodging:

Season:

☐ Spring ☐ Summer ☐ Fall ☐ Winter   Fee(s):   ☐ Free:

Favorite moment:

Sights:

Wildlife:

Popular attractions:

☐ Nunsting Village   ☐ The Haida Gwaii Watchmen
☐ K'uuna Llnagaay (Skedans)   ☐ Haida Longhouses
☐ Burnaby Narrows   ☐ Hotspring Island
☐ Anthony Island   ☐ Gwaay Guusdagang
☐ Windy Bay   ☐ Swan Bay Rediscovery Program
☐ The Legacy Pole   ☐ ....
☐ Mount Yatza   ☐ ....

of day(s) of visit

☐ 1 ☐ 2 ☐ 3 ☐ 3+

Overall Experience

10

Journal, Sketch, Photo & Passport Page

PHOTO & STAMP HERE

Essential Gear

- [ ] This Book!
- [ ] Park Map
- [ ] Camera
- [ ] Sweater
- [ ] Binoculars
- [ ] Magnifying Glass
- [ ] Insect Repellent
- [ ] Water Bottle
- [ ] Snacks
- [ ] Swimsuit
- [ ] Towel
- [ ] First Aid Kit
- [ ] Hat
- [ ] Sunblock
- [ ] Pen/pencil
- [ ] Backpack
- [ ] Field Guide
- [ ] Trash Bag
- [ ] ----------
- [ ] ----------
- [ ] ----------
- [ ] ----------
- [ ] ----------
- [ ] ----------
- [ ] ----------

- [ ] ----------
- [ ] ----------
- [ ] ----------
- [ ] ----------
- [ ] ----------
- [ ] ----------
- [ ] ----------
- [ ] ----------
- [ ] ----------
- [ ] ----------
- [ ] ----------
- [ ] ----------
- [ ] ----------
- [ ] ----------
- [ ] ----------
- [ ] ----------
- [ ] ----------
- [ ] ----------
- [ ] ----------
- [ ] ----------
- [ ] ----------
- [ ] ----------
- [ ] ----------
- [ ] ----------
- [ ] ----------

- [ ] ----------
- [ ] ----------
- [ ] ----------
- [ ] ----------
- [ ] ----------
- [ ] ----------
- [ ] ----------
- [ ] ----------
- [ ] ----------
- [ ] ----------
- [ ] ----------
- [ ] ----------
- [ ] ----------
- [ ] ----------
- [ ] ----------
- [ ] ----------
- [ ] ----------
- [ ] ----------
- [ ] ----------
- [ ] ----------
- [ ] ----------
- [ ] ----------
- [ ] ----------
- [ ] ----------
- [ ] ----------

Ivvavik

Yukon | Est.: 1984 | Area (km²): 10,168 | Coord.: 69° 5′ 0″ N, 139° 30′ 0″ W

Date: Temp.:

Who I went with:

Weather: ☀ ⛅ ☁ ❄ 🌧 💨
⬜ ⬜ ⬜ ⬜ ⬜ ⬜

Lodging:

Season:

⬜ Spring ⬜ Summer ⬜ Fall ⬜ Winter

Fee(s):   ⬜ Free:

Favorite moment:

Sights:

Wildlife:

Popular attractions:

⬜ Margaret Lake
⬜ Komakuk Beach
⬜ Sheep Creek
⬜ Halfway to Heaven Trail
⬜ Babbage Falls
⬜ The Dragon's Gate
⬜ Stokes Point

⬜ Firth River - Arctic Ocean Raft
⬜ Engigstiack Knoll
⬜ Inspiration Point
⬜ ....
⬜ ....
⬜ ....
⬜ ....

of day(s) of visit

⬜ 1 ⬜ 2 ⬜ 3 ⬜ 3+

Overall Experience

―――
10

Journal, Sketch, Photo & Passport Page

PHOTO & STAMP HERE

Essential Gear

- ☐ This Book!
- ☐ Park Map
- ☐ Camera
- ☐ Sweater
- ☐ Binoculars
- ☐ Magnifying Glass
- ☐ Insect Repellent
- ☐ Water Bottle
- ☐ Snacks
- ☐ Swimsuit
- ☐ Towel
- ☐ First Aid Kit
- ☐ Hat
- ☐ Sunblock
- ☐ Pen/pencil
- ☐ Backpack
- ☐ Field Guide
- ☐ Trash Bag
- ☐ ----------
- ☐ ----------
- ☐ ----------
- ☐ ----------
- ☐ ----------
- ☐ ----------
- ☐ ----------

- ☐ ----------
- ☐ ----------
- ☐ ----------
- ☐ ----------
- ☐ ----------
- ☐ ----------
- ☐ ----------
- ☐ ----------
- ☐ ----------
- ☐ ----------
- ☐ ----------
- ☐ ----------
- ☐ ----------
- ☐ ----------
- ☐ ----------
- ☐ ----------
- ☐ ----------
- ☐ ----------
- ☐ ----------
- ☐ ----------
- ☐ ----------
- ☐ ----------
- ☐ ----------
- ☐ ----------
- ☐ ----------

- ☐ ----------
- ☐ ----------
- ☐ ----------
- ☐ ----------
- ☐ ----------
- ☐ ----------
- ☐ ----------
- ☐ ----------
- ☐ ----------
- ☐ ----------
- ☐ ----------
- ☐ ----------
- ☐ ----------
- ☐ ----------
- ☐ ----------
- ☐ ----------
- ☐ ----------
- ☐ ----------
- ☐ ----------
- ☐ ----------
- ☐ ----------
- ☐ ----------
- ☐ ----------
- ☐ ----------
- ☐ ----------

Jasper

Alberta | Est.: 1907 | Area (km²): 11,228 | Coord.: 52° 59′ 0″ N, 118° 6′ 0″ W

Date: Temp.:   Who I went with:

Weather: ☼ ⛅ ☁ ❄ 🌧 💨

◻ ◻ ◻ ◻ ◻ ◻   Lodging:

Season:

◻ Spring ◻ Summer ◻ Fall ◻ Winter   Fee(s):   ◻ Free:

Favorite moment:

Sights:

Wildlife:

Popular attractions:

◻ Jasper Discovery Trail   ◻ Sunwapta Falls and Canyon
◻ Traction Kiting   ◻ The Icefields Parkway
◻ Miette Hot Springs   ◻ The Glacier Skywalk
◻ Pyramid Lake   ◻ Tangle Creek Falls
◻ Athabasca Falls   ◻ Goat Lick
◻ Athabasca Glacier   ◻ Geocaching
◻ Maligne Canyon   ◻ The Jasper Planetarium

# of day(s) of visit

◯ 1 ◯ 2 ◯ 3 ◯ 3+

Overall Experience

10

Journal, Sketch, Photo & Passport Page

PHOTO & STAMP HERE

Essential Gear

- ☐ This Book!
- ☐ Park Map
- ☐ Camera
- ☐ Sweater
- ☐ Binoculars
- ☐ Magnifying Glass
- ☐ Insect Repellent
- ☐ Water Bottle
- ☐ Snacks
- ☐ Swimsuit
- ☐ Towel
- ☐ First Aid Kit
- ☐ Hat
- ☐ Sunblock
- ☐ Pen/pencil
- ☐ Backpack
- ☐ Field Guide
- ☐ Trash Bag
- ☐ ----------
- ☐ ----------
- ☐ ----------
- ☐ ----------
- ☐ ----------
- ☐ ----------
- ☐ ----------

Kejimkujik

Nova Scotia | Est.: 1967 | Area (km²): 404 | Coord.: 44° 23' 10" N, 65° 17' 35" W

Date: Temp.:

Who I went with:

Weather: ☀ ⛅ 🌧 ❄ ⛈ 💨

⬜ ⬜ ⬜ ⬜ ⬜ ⬜

Lodging:

Season:

⬜ Spring ⬜ Summer ⬜ Fall ⬜ Winter

Fee(s):   ⬜ Free:

Favorite moment:

Sights:

Wildlife:

Popular attractions:

⬜ Mill Falls   ⬜ Hemlocks And Hardwoods Trail
⬜ Merrymakedge Beach   ⬜ Gold Mines Trail
⬜ Kejimkujik Lake   ⬜ The Wejisqalia'ti'k – Mi'kmaw
⬜ Ukme'k Trail   ⬜ Mersey River Trail
⬜ Grafton Woods Loop   ⬜ The Birch Bark Canoe Project
⬜ Petroglyph Tour   ⬜ Geocaching
⬜ Harbour Rocks Trail   ⬜ Jeremy's Bay Campground

# of day(s) of visit

⭕1 ⭕2 ⭕3 ⭕3+

Overall Experience

10

Journal, Sketch, Photo & Passport Page

PHOTO & STAMP
HERE

Essential Gear

- [ ] This Book!
- [ ] Park Map
- [ ] Camera
- [ ] Sweater
- [ ] Binoculars
- [ ] Magnifying Glass
- [ ] Insect Repellent
- [ ] Water Bottle
- [ ] Snacks
- [ ] Swimsuit
- [ ] Towel
- [ ] First Aid Kit
- [ ] Hat
- [ ] Sunblock
- [ ] Pen/pencil
- [ ] Backpack
- [ ] Field Guide
- [ ] Trash Bag
- [ ] ----------
- [ ] ----------
- [ ] ----------
- [ ] ----------
- [ ] ----------
- [ ] ----------
- [ ] ----------

Kluane

Yukon | Est.: 1976 | Area (km²): 22,013 | Coord.: 60° 27′ 13″ N, 137° 49′ 45″ W

Date: Temp.:

Who I went with:

Weather: ☀ ⛅ ☁ ❄ 🌧 💨
⬭ ⬭ ⬭ ⬭ ⬭ ⬭

Lodging:

Season:

⬭ Spring   ⬭ Summer   ⬭ Fall   ⬭ Winter

Fee(s):   ⬭ Free:

Favorite moment:

Sights:

Wildlife:

Popular attractions:

⬭ Paddling Kathleen Lake   ⬭ Alder Creek Valley
⬭ The King's Throne   ⬭ Observation Mountain
⬭ St. Elias Lake Trail   ⬭ Kaskawulsh Glacier
⬭ Ice Cave Trail   ⬭ Bullion Creek
⬭ Alsek River Rafting   ⬭ Kokanee Trail
⬭ Sheep Creek Trail   ⬭ Lowell Glacier
⬭ Cottonwood Trail   ⬭ Tatshenshini River Rafting

of day(s) of visit

◯1 ◯2 ◯3 ◯3+

Overall Experience

10

Journal, Sketch, Photo & Passport Page

PHOTO & STAMP HERE

Essential Gear

- [ ] This Book!
- [ ] Park Map
- [ ] Camera
- [ ] Sweater
- [ ] Binoculars
- [ ] Magnifying Glass
- [ ] Insect Repellent
- [ ] Water Bottle
- [ ] Snacks
- [ ] Swimsuit
- [ ] Towel
- [ ] First Aid Kit
- [ ] Hat
- [ ] Sunblock
- [ ] Pen/pencil
- [ ] Backpack
- [ ] Field Guide
- [ ] Trash Bag
- [ ] -----------
- [ ] -----------
- [ ] -----------
- [ ] -----------
- [ ] -----------
- [ ] -----------
- [ ] -----------

Kootenay

British Columbia | Est.: 1920 | Area (km²): 1,406 | Coord.: 50° 57′ 0″ N, 116° 2′ 0″ W

Date: Temp.:

Weather: ☀ ⛅ 🌧 ❄ 🌦 💨
⬭ ⬭ ⬭ ⬭ ⬭ ⬭

Who I went with:

Lodging:

Season:

⬭ Spring ⬭ Summer ⬭ Fall ⬭ Winter

Fee(s):   ⬭ Free:

Favorite moment:

Sights:

Wildlife:

Popular attractions:

⬭ Radium Hot Springs   ⬭ Banff-Windermere Highway
⬭ Numa Falls   ⬭ Sinclair Canyon
⬭ Stanley Glacier Trail   ⬭ The Redwall Fault
⬭ The Paint Pots   ⬭ McLeod Meadows Day Use Area
⬭ Marble Canyon   ⬭ Dog Lake Trail
⬭ Stanley Glacier Trail   ⬭ Kootenay Valley Viewpoint
⬭ Burgess Shale Fossils   ⬭ Geocache Challenge

of day(s) of visit

◯1 ◯2 ◯3 ◯3+

Overall Experience

_____
10

Journal, Sketch, Photo & Passport Page

PHOTO & STAMP HERE

Essential Gear

- ☐ This Book!
- ☐ Park Map
- ☐ Camera
- ☐ Sweater
- ☐ Binoculars
- ☐ Magnifying Glass
- ☐ Insect Repellent
- ☐ Water Bottle
- ☐ Snacks
- ☐ Swimsuit
- ☐ Towel
- ☐ First Aid Kit
- ☐ Hat
- ☐ Sunblock
- ☐ Pen/pencil
- ☐ Backpack
- ☐ Field Guide
- ☐ Trash Bag
- ☐ ----------
- ☐ ----------
- ☐ ----------
- ☐ ----------
- ☐ ----------
- ☐ ----------
- ☐ ----------

- ☐ ----------
- ☐ ----------
- ☐ ----------
- ☐ ----------
- ☐ ----------
- ☐ ----------
- ☐ ----------
- ☐ ----------
- ☐ ----------
- ☐ ----------
- ☐ ----------
- ☐ ----------
- ☐ ----------
- ☐ ----------
- ☐ ----------
- ☐ ----------
- ☐ ----------
- ☐ ----------
- ☐ ----------
- ☐ ----------
- ☐ ----------
- ☐ ----------
- ☐ ----------
- ☐ ----------
- ☐ ----------

- ☐ ----------
- ☐ ----------
- ☐ ----------
- ☐ ----------
- ☐ ----------
- ☐ ----------
- ☐ ----------
- ☐ ----------
- ☐ ----------
- ☐ ----------
- ☐ ----------
- ☐ ----------
- ☐ ----------
- ☐ ----------
- ☐ ----------
- ☐ ----------
- ☐ ----------
- ☐ ----------
- ☐ ----------
- ☐ ----------
- ☐ ----------
- ☐ ----------
- ☐ ----------
- ☐ ----------
- ☐ ----------

Kouchibouguac

New Brunswick | Est.: 1969 | Area (km²): 238 | Coord.: 46° 51′ 30″ N, 64° 58′ 30″ W

Date: Temp.:

Weather: ☀ ⛅ ☁ ❄ 🌧 💨
⬜ ⬜ ⬜ ⬜ ⬜ ⬜

Season:

⬜ Spring   ⬜ Summer   ⬜ Fall   ⬜ Winter

Who I went with:

Lodging:

Fee(s):   ⬜ Free:

Favorite moment:

Sights:

Wildlife:

Popular attractions:

⬜ Kellys Beach Boardwalk   ⬜ Beaver Self-Guided Trail

⬜ Kellys Beach Canteen   ⬜ Pijeboogwek Winter Area

⬜ Callanders Beach   ⬜ Softshell Clam Fishing

⬜ Mi'gmag - Cedar Trail   ⬜ Claire-Fontaine Trail

⬜ The Wigwam Gathering   ⬜ The Voyageur Canoe Experience

⬜ Pines Trail   ⬜ Pointe A Maxime Canoe Camp

⬜ Bog Trail   ⬜ Geocache Challenge

# of day(s) of visit

○1 ○2 ○3 ○3+

Overall Experience

10

Journal, Sketch, Photo & Passport Page

PHOTO & STAMP HERE

Essential Gear

- [ ] This Book!
- [ ] Park Map
- [ ] Camera
- [ ] Sweater
- [ ] Binoculars
- [ ] Magnifying Glass
- [ ] Insect Repellent
- [ ] Water Bottle
- [ ] Snacks
- [ ] Swimsuit
- [ ] Towel
- [ ] First Aid Kit
- [ ] Hat
- [ ] Sunblock
- [ ] Pen/pencil
- [ ] Backpack
- [ ] Field Guide
- [ ] Trash Bag
- [ ] _____
- [ ] _____
- [ ] _____
- [ ] _____
- [ ] _____
- [ ] _____
- [ ] _____

- [ ] _____
- [ ] _____
- [ ] _____
- [ ] _____
- [ ] _____
- [ ] _____
- [ ] _____
- [ ] _____
- [ ] _____
- [ ] _____
- [ ] _____
- [ ] _____
- [ ] _____
- [ ] _____
- [ ] _____
- [ ] _____
- [ ] _____
- [ ] _____
- [ ] _____
- [ ] _____
- [ ] _____
- [ ] _____
- [ ] _____
- [ ] _____
- [ ] _____

- [ ] _____
- [ ] _____
- [ ] _____
- [ ] _____
- [ ] _____
- [ ] _____
- [ ] _____
- [ ] _____
- [ ] _____
- [ ] _____
- [ ] _____
- [ ] _____
- [ ] _____
- [ ] _____
- [ ] _____
- [ ] _____
- [ ] _____
- [ ] _____
- [ ] _____
- [ ] _____
- [ ] _____
- [ ] _____
- [ ] _____
- [ ] _____
- [ ] _____

La Mauricie

Quebec | Est.: 1970 | Area (km²): 536 | Coord.: 46° 48′ 0″ N, 72° 58′ 0″ W

Date: Temp.:   Who I went with:

Weather: ☀ ⛅ 🌧 ❄ 🌦 💨
☐ ☐ ☐ ☐ ☐ ☐   Lodging:

Season:

☐ Spring ☐ Summer ☐ Fall ☐ Winter   Fee(s):   ☐ Free:

Favorite moment:

Sights:

Wildlife:

Popular attractions:

☐ Les Cascades Trail   ☐ Beaver Self-Guided Trail
☐ Édouard Lake   ☐ Pijeboogwek Winter Area
☐ Waber Falls   ☐ The Aqua Trek
☐ Caribou Lake   ☐ Rivière à la Pêche Bike Trails
☐ Le Passage Lookout   ☐ Domaine Wabenaki-Andrew
☐ Mekinac Floating-Bridge   ☐ The Shewenegan Picnic Area
☐ Mekinac Floating-Bridge   ☐ Solitaire Lake Trail

of day(s) of visit

○1 ○2 ○3 ○3+

Overall Experience

10

Journal, Sketch, Photo & Passport Page

PHOTO & STAMP HERE

Essential Gear

- ☐ This Book!
- ☐ Park Map
- ☐ Camera
- ☐ Sweater
- ☐ Binoculars
- ☐ Magnifying Glass
- ☐ Insect Repellent
- ☐ Water Bottle
- ☐ Snacks
- ☐ Swimsuit
- ☐ Towel
- ☐ First Aid Kit
- ☐ Hat
- ☐ Sunblock
- ☐ Pen/pencil
- ☐ Backpack
- ☐ Field Guide
- ☐ Trash Bag
- ☐ _____
- ☐ _____
- ☐ _____
- ☐ _____
- ☐ _____
- ☐ _____
- ☐ _____

- ☐ _____
- ☐ _____
- ☐ _____
- ☐ _____
- ☐ _____
- ☐ _____
- ☐ _____
- ☐ _____
- ☐ _____
- ☐ _____
- ☐ _____
- ☐ _____
- ☐ _____
- ☐ _____
- ☐ _____
- ☐ _____
- ☐ _____
- ☐ _____
- ☐ _____
- ☐ _____
- ☐ _____
- ☐ _____
- ☐ _____
- ☐ _____
- ☐ _____

- ☐ _____
- ☐ _____
- ☐ _____
- ☐ _____
- ☐ _____
- ☐ _____
- ☐ _____
- ☐ _____
- ☐ _____
- ☐ _____
- ☐ _____
- ☐ _____
- ☐ _____
- ☐ _____
- ☐ _____
- ☐ _____
- ☐ _____
- ☐ _____
- ☐ _____
- ☐ _____
- ☐ _____
- ☐ _____
- ☐ _____
- ☐ _____
- ☐ _____

Mingan Archipelago

Quebec | Est.: 1984 | Area (km²): 151 | Coord.: 50° 13′ 0″ N, 63° 10′ 0″ W

Date:　　　　　Temp.:

Who I went with:

Weather: ☀ ⛅ ☁ ❄ 🌧 💨
☐ ☐ ☐ ☐ ☐ ☐

Lodging:

Season:

☐ Spring ☐ Summer ☐ Fall ☐ Winter

Fee(s):　　　　　　　☐ Free:

Favorite moment:

Sights:

Wildlife:

Popular attractions:

☐ Bonne Femme Monolith
☐ Poète Jomphe Trail
☐ Samuel Trail
☐ Capailloux Hike
☐ La Montagnaise Monolith
☐ Les Falaises Trail
☐ Les Cypripèdes Trail

☐ Anse des Érosions Trail
☐ Campanules Trail
☐ The Lightkeeper's Cottage
☐ Campanules Trail
☐ Boreal Flavours Guided Hike
☐ The Historic Basque Ovens
☐ ....

# of day(s) of visit

☐1 ☐2 ☐3 ☐3+

Overall Experience

____
10

Journal, Sketch, Photo & Passport Page

PHOTO & STAMP HERE

Essential Gear

- ☐ This Book!
- ☐ Park Map
- ☐ Camera
- ☐ Sweater
- ☐ Binoculars
- ☐ Magnifying Glass
- ☐ Insect Repellent
- ☐ Water Bottle
- ☐ Snacks
- ☐ Swimsuit
- ☐ Towel
- ☐ First Aid Kit
- ☐ Hat
- ☐ Sunblock
- ☐ Pen/pencil
- ☐ Backpack
- ☐ Field Guide
- ☐ Trash Bag
- ☐ ----------
- ☐ ----------
- ☐ ----------
- ☐ ----------
- ☐ ----------
- ☐ ----------
- ☐ ----------

Mount Revelstoke

British Columbia | Est.: 1914 | Area (km²): 260 | Coord.: 51° 6′ 0″ N, 118° 4′ 0″ W

Date: Temp.:

Weather: ☀ ⛅ 🌧 ❄ 🌦 💨
☐ ☐ ☐ ☐ ☐ ☐

Season:
☐ Spring ☐ Summer ☐ Fall ☐ Winter

Who I went with:

Lodging:

Fee(s):   ☐ Free:

Favorite moment:

Sights:

Wildlife:

Popular attractions:

☐ Meadows in Sky Parkway   ☐ The Inspiration Woods Trail

☐ Eva Lake Trail   ☐ Beaver Lodge Kids Bike Park

☐ The First Footsteps Trail   ☐ Skunk Cabbage Boardwalk

☐ Koo Koo Sint Trail   ☐ The Nels Nelsen Ski Jump

☐ Balsam Lake   ☐ Geocaching Challenge

☐ The Monashee Lookout   ☐ Mount Revelstoke Trail

☐ Giant Cedars Boardwalk   ☐ Historic Fire Lookout

# of day(s) of visit

○1 ○2 ○3 ○3+

Overall Experience

10

Journal, Sketch, Photo & Passport Page

PHOTO & STAMP HERE

Essential Gear

- ☐ This Book!
- ☐ Park Map
- ☐ Camera
- ☐ Sweater
- ☐ Binoculars
- ☐ Magnifying Glass
- ☐ Insect Repellent
- ☐ Water Bottle
- ☐ Snacks
- ☐ Swimsuit
- ☐ Towel
- ☐ First Aid Kit
- ☐ Hat
- ☐ Sunblock
- ☐ Pen/pencil
- ☐ Backpack
- ☐ Field Guide
- ☐ Trash Bag
- ☐ ----------
- ☐ ----------
- ☐ ----------
- ☐ ----------
- ☐ ----------
- ☐ ----------
- ☐ ----------

- ☐ ----------
- ☐ ----------
- ☐ ----------
- ☐ ----------
- ☐ ----------
- ☐ ----------
- ☐ ----------
- ☐ ----------
- ☐ ----------
- ☐ ----------
- ☐ ----------
- ☐ ----------
- ☐ ----------
- ☐ ----------
- ☐ ----------
- ☐ ----------
- ☐ ----------
- ☐ ----------
- ☐ ----------
- ☐ ----------
- ☐ ----------
- ☐ ----------
- ☐ ----------
- ☐ ----------
- ☐ ----------

- ☐ ----------
- ☐ ----------
- ☐ ----------
- ☐ ----------
- ☐ ----------
- ☐ ----------
- ☐ ----------
- ☐ ----------
- ☐ ----------
- ☐ ----------
- ☐ ----------
- ☐ ----------
- ☐ ----------
- ☐ ----------
- ☐ ----------
- ☐ ----------
- ☐ ----------
- ☐ ----------
- ☐ ----------
- ☐ ----------
- ☐ ----------
- ☐ ----------
- ☐ ----------
- ☐ ----------
- ☐ ----------

Nááts'įhch'oh

Northwest Territories | Est.: 2014 | Area (km²): 4,850 | Coord.: 62° 15' 0″ N, 128° 15' 0″ W

Date: Temp.:   Who I went with:

Weather: ☀ ⛅ 🌧 ❄ 🌦 💨
◻ ◻ ◻ ◻ ◻ ◻   Lodging:

Season:

◻ Spring ◻ Summer ◻ Fall ◻ Winter | Fee(s):   ◻ Free:

Favorite moment:

Sights:

Wildlife:

Popular attractions:

◻ Divide Lake
◻ Broken Skull River
◻ Swallow Falls
◻ Three Valley Confluence
◻ Broken Skull Hot Springs
◻ Little Nahanni River
◻ South Nahanni River

◻ Rabbitkettle Lake
◻ Backbone Lake
◻ Grizzly Bear Hot Springs
◻ O'Grady Lake
◻ The Broken Heart Plateau
◻ Margaret Lake
◻ The Triple Header Badge

# of day(s) of visit

○1 ○2 ○3 ○3+

Overall Experience

10

Journal, Sketch, Photo & Passport Page

PHOTO & STAMP
HERE

Essential Gear

- ☐ This Book!
- ☐ Park Map
- ☐ Camera
- ☐ Sweater
- ☐ Binoculars
- ☐ Magnifying Glass
- ☐ Insect Repellent
- ☐ Water Bottle
- ☐ Snacks
- ☐ Swimsuit
- ☐ Towel
- ☐ First Aid Kit
- ☐ Hat
- ☐ Sunblock
- ☐ Pen/pencil
- ☐ Backpack
- ☐ Field Guide
- ☐ Trash Bag
- ☐ -----------
- ☐ -----------
- ☐ -----------
- ☐ -----------
- ☐ -----------
- ☐ -----------
- ☐ -----------

- ☐ -----------
- ☐ -----------
- ☐ -----------
- ☐ -----------
- ☐ -----------
- ☐ -----------
- ☐ -----------
- ☐ -----------
- ☐ -----------
- ☐ -----------
- ☐ -----------
- ☐ -----------
- ☐ -----------
- ☐ -----------
- ☐ -----------
- ☐ -----------
- ☐ -----------
- ☐ -----------
- ☐ -----------
- ☐ -----------
- ☐ -----------
- ☐ -----------
- ☐ -----------
- ☐ -----------
- ☐ -----------

- ☐ -----------
- ☐ -----------
- ☐ -----------
- ☐ -----------
- ☐ -----------
- ☐ -----------
- ☐ -----------
- ☐ -----------
- ☐ -----------
- ☐ -----------
- ☐ -----------
- ☐ -----------
- ☐ -----------
- ☐ -----------
- ☐ -----------
- ☐ -----------
- ☐ -----------
- ☐ -----------
- ☐ -----------
- ☐ -----------
- ☐ -----------
- ☐ -----------
- ☐ -----------
- ☐ -----------
- ☐ -----------

Nahanni

Northwest Territories | Est.: 1972 | Area (km²): 30,050 | Coord.: 61° 36′ 0″ N, 125° 41′ 6″ W

Date: Temp.:

Weather: ☀ ⛅ 🌧 ❄ 🌦 💨
☐ ☐ ☐ ☐ ☐ ☐

Season:
☐ Spring ☐ Summer ☐ Fall ☐ Winter

Who I went with:

Lodging:

Fee(s):   ☐ Free:

Favorite moment:

Sights:

Wildlife:

Popular attractions:

☐ South Nahanni River   ☐ Fairy Meadows
☐ Virginia Falls   ☐ Rabbitkettle Hot Springs
☐ Sunblood Mountain   ☐ Kraus Hot Springs
☐ The Gate   ☐ Cirque of the Unclimbables
☐ The Pulpit Rock   ☐ Lotus-Flower-Tower Peak
☐ Tl'ogotsho Plateau   ☐ Ram Creek Trail
☐ Vampire Peaks   ☐ Hole-in-the-Wall Lake

# of day(s) of visit
○1 ○2 ○3 ○3+

Overall Experience

10

Journal, Sketch, Photo & Passport Page

PHOTO & STAMP HERE

Essential Gear

- [ ] This Book!
- [ ] Park Map
- [ ] Camera
- [ ] Sweater
- [ ] Binoculars
- [ ] Magnifying Glass
- [ ] Insect Repellent
- [ ] Water Bottle
- [ ] Snacks
- [ ] Swimsuit
- [ ] Towel
- [ ] First Aid Kit
- [ ] Hat
- [ ] Sunblock
- [ ] Pen/pencil
- [ ] Backpack
- [ ] Field Guide
- [ ] Trash Bag
- [ ] _____
- [ ] _____
- [ ] _____
- [ ] _____
- [ ] _____
- [ ] _____
- [ ] _____

- [ ] _____
- [ ] _____
- [ ] _____
- [ ] _____
- [ ] _____
- [ ] _____
- [ ] _____
- [ ] _____
- [ ] _____
- [ ] _____
- [ ] _____
- [ ] _____
- [ ] _____
- [ ] _____
- [ ] _____
- [ ] _____
- [ ] _____
- [ ] _____
- [ ] _____
- [ ] _____
- [ ] _____
- [ ] _____

- [ ] _____
- [ ] _____
- [ ] _____
- [ ] _____
- [ ] _____
- [ ] _____
- [ ] _____
- [ ] _____
- [ ] _____
- [ ] _____
- [ ] _____
- [ ] _____
- [ ] _____
- [ ] _____
- [ ] _____
- [ ] _____
- [ ] _____
- [ ] _____
- [ ] _____
- [ ] _____
- [ ] _____
- [ ] _____

Pacific Rim

British Columbia | Est.: 1970 | Area (km²): 511 | Coord.: 48° 59′ 0″ N, 125° 40′ 0″ W

Date: Temp.:

Who I went with:

Weather: ☼ ⛅ ☁ ❄ 🌧 💨
⬜ ⬜ ⬜ ⬜ ⬜ ⬜

Lodging:

Season:

⬜ Spring ⬜ Summer ⬜ Fall ⬜ Winter

Fee(s):   ⬜ Free:

Favorite moment:

Sights:

Wildlife:

Popular attractions:

⬜ Wickaninnish Beach
⬜ Long Beach
⬜ Kwisitis Visitor Centre
⬜ Nuu-chah-nulth Trail
⬜ Rainforest Trail
⬜ Radar Hill
⬜ South Beach Trail

⬜ Shorepine Bog Trail
⬜ The Wickanninish Centre
⬜ Broken Group Islands
⬜ Benson Island
⬜ Cape Beale Headlands
⬜ Storm Watching
⬜ Geocaching Challenge

of day(s) of visit

⭕1 ⭕2 ⭕3 ⭕3+

Overall Experience

10

Journal, Sketch, Photo & Passport Page

PHOTO & STAMP HERE

Essential Gear

- [ ] This Book!
- [ ] Park Map
- [ ] Camera
- [ ] Sweater
- [ ] Binoculars
- [ ] Magnifying Glass
- [ ] Insect Repellent
- [ ] Water Bottle
- [ ] Snacks
- [ ] Swimsuit
- [ ] Towel
- [ ] First Aid Kit
- [ ] Hat
- [ ] Sunblock
- [ ] Pen/pencil
- [ ] Backpack
- [ ] Field Guide
- [ ] Trash Bag
- [ ] _____
- [ ] _____
- [ ] _____
- [ ] _____
- [ ] _____
- [ ] _____
- [ ] _____

Point Pelee

Ontario | Est.: 1918 | Area (km²): 15 | Coord.: 41° 58′ 0″ N, 82° 31′ 0″ W

Date: Temp.:

Weather: ☀ ⛅ 🌧 ❄ 🌦 💨
☐ ☐ ☐ ☐ ☐ ☐

Season:
☐ Spring ☐ Summer ☐ Fall ☐ Winter

Who I went with:

Lodging:

Fee(s):   ☐ Free:

Favorite moment:

Sights:

Wildlife:

Popular attractions:

☐ Marsh Boardwalk   ☐ DeLaurier Homestead & Trail
☐ Chinquapin Oak Trail   ☐ Northwest Beach Kids Area
☐ Woodland Nature Trail   ☐ Botham Tree Trail
☐ Redhead Pond   ☐ Spring Wildflower Walk
☐ East Cranberry Pond   ☐ Point Pelee Viewing Platform
☐ Point Pelee Birding Area   ☐ The Tip
☐ South Beach Trail   ☐ Geocaching Adventure

# of day(s) of visit
○ 1 ○ 2 ○ 3 ○ 3+

Overall Experience

10

83

Journal, Sketch, Photo & Passport Page

PHOTO & STAMP HERE

Essential Gear

- [ ] This Book!
- [ ] Park Map
- [ ] Camera
- [ ] Sweater
- [ ] Binoculars
- [ ] Magnifying Glass
- [ ] Insect Repellent
- [ ] Water Bottle
- [ ] Snacks
- [ ] Swimsuit
- [ ] Towel
- [ ] First Aid Kit
- [ ] Hat
- [ ] Sunblock
- [ ] Pen/pencil
- [ ] Backpack
- [ ] Field Guide
- [ ] Trash Bag
- [ ] _____
- [ ] _____
- [ ] _____
- [ ] _____
- [ ] _____
- [ ] _____
- [ ] _____

- [ ] _____
- [ ] _____
- [ ] _____
- [ ] _____
- [ ] _____
- [ ] _____
- [ ] _____
- [ ] _____
- [ ] _____
- [ ] _____
- [ ] _____
- [ ] _____
- [ ] _____
- [ ] _____
- [ ] _____
- [ ] _____
- [ ] _____
- [ ] _____
- [ ] _____
- [ ] _____
- [ ] _____
- [ ] _____
- [ ] _____
- [ ] _____
- [ ] _____

- [ ] _____
- [ ] _____
- [ ] _____
- [ ] _____
- [ ] _____
- [ ] _____
- [ ] _____
- [ ] _____
- [ ] _____
- [ ] _____
- [ ] _____
- [ ] _____
- [ ] _____
- [ ] _____
- [ ] _____
- [ ] _____
- [ ] _____
- [ ] _____
- [ ] _____
- [ ] _____
- [ ] _____
- [ ] _____
- [ ] _____
- [ ] _____
- [ ] _____

Prince Albert

Saskatchewan | Est.: 1927 | Area (km²): 3,874 | Coord.: 53° 57′ 48″ N, 106° 22′ 12″ W

Date:　　　　　Temp.:

Who I went with:

Weather: ☀ ⛅ ☁ ❄ 🌧 💨
⬭ ⬭ ⬭ ⬭ ⬭ ⬭

Lodging:

Season:

⬭ Spring ⬭ Summer ⬭ Fall ⬭ Winter

Fee(s): ⬭ Free:

Favorite moment:

Sights:

Wildlife:

Popular attractions:

⬭ Waskesiu Lake　　　⬭ Valleyview Trail Network
⬭ Narrows Beach　　　⬭ Freight Tait Springs Trail
⬭ Mud Creek Trail　　⬭ Spruce River Highlands Trail
⬭ Grey Owl's Cabin　　⬭ Boundary Bog Trail
⬭ Paignton Beach　　　⬭ Waskesiu's Lobstick Golf Course
⬭ Elk Trail　　　　　　⬭ Treebeard Trail
⬭ The South Bay　　　⬭ Geocaching Adventure

# of day(s) of visit

◯1 ◯2 ◯3 ◯3+

Overall Experience

—— 10

86

Journal, Sketch, Photo & Passport Page

PHOTO & STAMP HERE

Essential Gear

- ☐ This Book!
- ☐ Park Map
- ☐ Camera
- ☐ Sweater
- ☐ Binoculars
- ☐ Magnifying Glass
- ☐ Insect Repellent
- ☐ Water Bottle
- ☐ Snacks
- ☐ Swimsuit
- ☐ Towel
- ☐ First Aid Kit
- ☐ Hat
- ☐ Sunblock
- ☐ Pen/pencil
- ☐ Backpack
- ☐ Field Guide
- ☐ Trash Bag
- ☐ -----------
- ☐ -----------
- ☐ -----------
- ☐ -----------
- ☐ -----------
- ☐ -----------
- ☐ -----------

- ☐ -----------
- ☐ -----------
- ☐ -----------
- ☐ -----------
- ☐ -----------
- ☐ -----------
- ☐ -----------
- ☐ -----------
- ☐ -----------
- ☐ -----------
- ☐ -----------
- ☐ -----------
- ☐ -----------
- ☐ -----------
- ☐ -----------
- ☐ -----------
- ☐ -----------
- ☐ -----------
- ☐ -----------
- ☐ -----------
- ☐ -----------
- ☐ -----------
- ☐ -----------

- ☐ -----------
- ☐ -----------
- ☐ -----------
- ☐ -----------
- ☐ -----------
- ☐ -----------
- ☐ -----------
- ☐ -----------
- ☐ -----------
- ☐ -----------
- ☐ -----------
- ☐ -----------
- ☐ -----------
- ☐ -----------
- ☐ -----------
- ☐ -----------
- ☐ -----------
- ☐ -----------
- ☐ -----------
- ☐ -----------
- ☐ -----------
- ☐ -----------
- ☐ -----------

Prince Edward Island

Prince Edward Island | Est.: 1937 | Area (km²): 27 | Coord.: 46° 26′ 0″ N, 63° 12′ 0″ W

Date: Temp.:

Who I went with:

Weather: ☀ ⛅ ☁ ❄ 🌧 💨
⬜ ⬜ ⬜ ⬜ ⬜ ⬜

Lodging:

Season:

⬜ Spring ⬜ Summer ⬜ Fall ⬜ Winter

Fee(s):   ⬜ Free:

Favorite moment:

Sights:

Wildlife:

Popular attractions:

⬜ Cavendish Beach
⬜ Brackley Beach
⬜ Gulf of St. Lawrence
⬜ North Rustico Beach
⬜ Greenwich Dunes Trail
⬜ Cavendish Cliffs
⬜ Green Gables Golf Club

⬜ Greenwich Interpretation Centre
⬜ Cavendish Dunelands Trail
⬜ The Gulf Shore Parkway
⬜ Green Gables Heritage Place
⬜ Dalvay-by-the-Sea Hotel
⬜ Havre Saint Pierre Trail
⬜ Geocaching Adventure

# of day(s) of visit

⬜1 ⬜2 ⬜3 ⬜3+

Overall Experience

——
10

Journal, Sketch, Photo & Passport Page

PHOTO & STAMP HERE

Essential Gear

- ☐ This Book!
- ☐ Park Map
- ☐ Camera
- ☐ Sweater
- ☐ Binoculars
- ☐ Magnifying Glass
- ☐ Insect Repellent
- ☐ Water Bottle
- ☐ Snacks
- ☐ Swimsuit
- ☐ Towel
- ☐ First Aid Kit
- ☐ Hat
- ☐ Sunblock
- ☐ Pen/pencil
- ☐ Backpack
- ☐ Field Guide
- ☐ Trash Bag
- ☐ ----------
- ☐ ----------
- ☐ ----------
- ☐ ----------
- ☐ ----------
- ☐ ----------
- ☐ ----------

- ☐ ----------
- ☐ ----------
- ☐ ----------
- ☐ ----------
- ☐ ----------
- ☐ ----------
- ☐ ----------
- ☐ ----------
- ☐ ----------
- ☐ ----------
- ☐ ----------
- ☐ ----------
- ☐ ----------
- ☐ ----------
- ☐ ----------
- ☐ ----------
- ☐ ----------
- ☐ ----------
- ☐ ----------
- ☐ ----------
- ☐ ----------
- ☐ ----------
- ☐ ----------
- ☐ ----------
- ☐ ----------

- ☐ ----------
- ☐ ----------
- ☐ ----------
- ☐ ----------
- ☐ ----------
- ☐ ----------
- ☐ ----------
- ☐ ----------
- ☐ ----------
- ☐ ----------
- ☐ ----------
- ☐ ----------
- ☐ ----------
- ☐ ----------
- ☐ ----------
- ☐ ----------
- ☐ ----------
- ☐ ----------
- ☐ ----------
- ☐ ----------
- ☐ ----------
- ☐ ----------
- ☐ ----------
- ☐ ----------
- ☐ ----------

Pukaskwa

Ontario | Est.: 1978 | Area (km²): 1,878 | Coord.: 48° 15′ 0″ N, 85° 55′ 0″ W

Date: Temp.:

Weather: ☀ ⛅ ☁ ❄ 🌧 💨
⬜ ⬜ ⬜ ⬜ ⬜ ⬜

Season:

⬜ Spring ⬜ Summer ⬜ Fall ⬜ Winter

Who I went with:

Lodging:

Fee(s):   ⬜ Free:

Favorite moment:

Sights:

Wildlife:

Popular attractions:

⬜ Lake Superior   ⬜ Anishinaabe Camp
⬜ Coastal Hiking Trail   ⬜ The Suspension Bridge Trail
⬜ The Visitor Center   ⬜ Chigamiwinigum Falls
⬜ Southern Headland Trail ⬜ Manito Miikna Trail
⬜ Boardwalk Beach Trail   ⬜ Pukaskwa Pits
⬜ Horseshoe Beach   ⬜ Bismose Kinoomagewnan Trail
⬜ Hattie Cove   ⬜ Geocaching Adventure

of day(s) of visit

◯1 ◯2 ◯3 ◯3+

Overall Experience

10

Journal, Sketch, Photo & Passport Page

PHOTO & STAMP
HERE

Essential Gear

- [ ] This Book!
- [ ] Park Map
- [ ] Camera
- [ ] Sweater
- [ ] Binoculars
- [ ] Magnifying Glass
- [ ] Insect Repellent
- [ ] Water Bottle
- [ ] Snacks
- [ ] Swimsuit
- [ ] Towel
- [ ] First Aid Kit
- [ ] Hat
- [ ] Sunblock
- [ ] Pen/pencil
- [ ] Backpack
- [ ] Field Guide
- [ ] Trash Bag
- [ ] _____
- [ ] _____
- [ ] _____
- [ ] _____
- [ ] _____
- [ ] _____
- [ ] _____

- [ ] _____
- [ ] _____
- [ ] _____
- [ ] _____
- [ ] _____
- [ ] _____
- [ ] _____
- [ ] _____
- [ ] _____
- [ ] _____
- [ ] _____
- [ ] _____
- [ ] _____
- [ ] _____
- [ ] _____
- [ ] _____
- [ ] _____
- [ ] _____
- [ ] _____
- [ ] _____
- [ ] _____
- [ ] _____
- [ ] _____
- [ ] _____
- [ ] _____

- [ ] _____
- [ ] _____
- [ ] _____
- [ ] _____
- [ ] _____
- [ ] _____
- [ ] _____
- [ ] _____
- [ ] _____
- [ ] _____
- [ ] _____
- [ ] _____
- [ ] _____
- [ ] _____
- [ ] _____
- [ ] _____
- [ ] _____
- [ ] _____
- [ ] _____
- [ ] _____
- [ ] _____
- [ ] _____
- [ ] _____
- [ ] _____
- [ ] _____

Qausuittuq

Nunavut | Est.: 2015 | Area (km²): 11,000 | Coord.: 76° 7′ 27″ N, 101° 1′ 52″ W

Date: Temp.:

Weather: ☀ ⛅ 🌧 ❄ 🌦 🌬
☐ ☐ ☐ ☐ ☐ ☐

Season:
☐ Spring ☐ Summer ☐ Fall ☐ Winter

Who I went with:

Lodging:

Fee(s):   ☐ Free:

Favorite moment:

Sights:

Wildlife:

Popular attractions:
☐ Bird Watching   ☐ ....
☐ Whale Watching   ☐ ....
☐ Hiking   ☐ ....
☐ Ski Touring   ☐ ....
☐ .... ☐ ....
☐ .... ☐ ....
☐ .... ☐ ....

# of day(s) of visit
◯1 ◯2 ◯3 ◯3+

Overall Experience

——
10

95

Journal, Sketch, Photo & Passport Page

PHOTO & STAMP HERE

Essential Gear

- [ ] This Book!
- [ ] Park Map
- [ ] Camera
- [ ] Sweater
- [ ] Binoculars
- [ ] Magnifying Glass
- [ ] Insect Repellent
- [ ] Water Bottle
- [ ] Snacks
- [ ] Swimsuit
- [ ] Towel
- [ ] First Aid Kit
- [ ] Hat
- [ ] Sunblock
- [ ] Pen/pencil
- [ ] Backpack
- [ ] Field Guide
- [ ] Trash Bag
- [ ] _____
- [ ] _____
- [ ] _____
- [ ] _____
- [ ] _____
- [ ] _____
- [ ] _____

- [ ] _____
- [ ] _____
- [ ] _____
- [ ] _____
- [ ] _____
- [ ] _____
- [ ] _____
- [ ] _____
- [ ] _____
- [ ] _____
- [ ] _____
- [ ] _____
- [ ] _____
- [ ] _____
- [ ] _____
- [ ] _____
- [ ] _____
- [ ] _____
- [ ] _____
- [ ] _____
- [ ] _____
- [ ] _____
- [ ] _____
- [ ] _____
- [ ] _____

- [ ] _____
- [ ] _____
- [ ] _____
- [ ] _____
- [ ] _____
- [ ] _____
- [ ] _____
- [ ] _____
- [ ] _____
- [ ] _____
- [ ] _____
- [ ] _____
- [ ] _____
- [ ] _____
- [ ] _____
- [ ] _____
- [ ] _____
- [ ] _____
- [ ] _____
- [ ] _____
- [ ] _____
- [ ] _____
- [ ] _____
- [ ] _____
- [ ] _____

Quttinirpaaq

Nunavut | Est.: 1988 | Area (km²): 37,775 | Coord.: 82° 13′ 0″ N, 72° 13′ 0″ W

Date: **Temp.:**   **Who I went with:**

Weather: ☀ ⛅ ☁ ❄ 🌧 💨
⬜ ⬜ ⬜ ⬜ ⬜ ⬜   **Lodging:**

Season:

⬜ Spring ⬜ Summer ⬜ Fall ⬜ Winter   **Fee(s):**   ⬜ **Free:**

Favorite moment:

Sights:

Wildlife:

Popular attractions:

⬜ Fort Conger Historic Site   ⬜ Ad Astra Ice Cap
⬜ Air Force Glacier   ⬜ The Viking Ice Cap
⬜ Fiala Glacier   ⬜ Ad Astra Ice Cap
⬜ Gull Glacier   ⬜ Lady Franklin Bay
⬜ Nunatak - Mount Barbeau   ⬜ Very River Valley
⬜ Lake Hazen Thermal Oasis   ⬜ MacDonald River
⬜ Tanquary Ford   ⬜ 24-Hour Daylight

# of day(s) of visit

⭕1 ⭕2 ⭕3 ⭕3+

Overall Experience

10

Journal, Sketch, Photo & Passport Page

PHOTO & STAMP HERE

Essential Gear

- ☐ This Book!
- ☐ Park Map
- ☐ Camera
- ☐ Sweater
- ☐ Binoculars
- ☐ Magnifying Glass
- ☐ Insect Repellent
- ☐ Water Bottle
- ☐ Snacks
- ☐ Swimsuit
- ☐ Towel
- ☐ First Aid Kit
- ☐ Hat
- ☐ Sunblock
- ☐ Pen/pencil
- ☐ Backpack
- ☐ Field Guide
- ☐ Trash Bag
- ☐ -----------
- ☐ -----------
- ☐ -----------
- ☐ -----------
- ☐ -----------
- ☐ -----------
- ☐ -----------

- ☐ -----------
- ☐ -----------
- ☐ -----------
- ☐ -----------
- ☐ -----------
- ☐ -----------
- ☐ -----------
- ☐ -----------
- ☐ -----------
- ☐ -----------
- ☐ -----------
- ☐ -----------
- ☐ -----------
- ☐ -----------
- ☐ -----------
- ☐ -----------
- ☐ -----------
- ☐ -----------
- ☐ -----------
- ☐ -----------
- ☐ -----------
- ☐ -----------
- ☐ -----------
- ☐ -----------
- ☐ -----------

- ☐ -----------
- ☐ -----------
- ☐ -----------
- ☐ -----------
- ☐ -----------
- ☐ -----------
- ☐ -----------
- ☐ -----------
- ☐ -----------
- ☐ -----------
- ☐ -----------
- ☐ -----------
- ☐ -----------
- ☐ -----------
- ☐ -----------
- ☐ -----------
- ☐ -----------
- ☐ -----------
- ☐ -----------
- ☐ -----------
- ☐ -----------
- ☐ -----------
- ☐ -----------
- ☐ -----------
- ☐ -----------

Riding Mountain

Manitoba | Est.: 1933 | Area (km²): 2,969 | Coord.: 50° 53′ 0″ N, 100° 15′ 0″ W

Date: Temp.:

Who I went with:

Weather: ☀️ ⛅ ☁️ ❄️ 🌧️ 💨
☐ ☐ ☐ ☐ ☐ ☐

Lodging:

Season:

☐ Spring ☐ Summer ☐ Fall ☐ Winter

Fee(s):   ☐ Free:

Favorite moment:

Sights:

Wildlife:

Popular attractions:

☐ Grey Owl's Cabin
☐ The Wishing Well
☐ Clear Lake Beach
☐ Clear Lake Golf Course
☐ Ominnik Marsh Trail
☐ The Historic East Gate
☐ Guided Boat Cruise

☐ Lake Audy Bison Enclosure
☐ Bald Hill Trail
☐ Kinosao Lake Free Canoe
☐ Burls and Bittersweet Trail
☐ Horse-Drawn-Wagon Trails
☐ Scuba Diving
☐ Geocaching Adventure

# of day(s) of visit

○1 ○2 ○3 ○3+

Overall Experience

10

Journal, Sketch, Photo & Passport Page

PHOTO & STAMP HERE

Essential Gear

- ☐ This Book!
- ☐ Park Map
- ☐ Camera
- ☐ Sweater
- ☐ Binoculars
- ☐ Magnifying Glass
- ☐ Insect Repellent
- ☐ Water Bottle
- ☐ Snacks
- ☐ Swimsuit
- ☐ Towel
- ☐ First Aid Kit
- ☐ Hat
- ☐ Sunblock
- ☐ Pen/pencil
- ☐ Backpack
- ☐ Field Guide
- ☐ Trash Bag

Rouge

Ontario | Est.: 2015 | Area (km²): 75 | Coord.: 43° 55′ 58″ N, 79° 13′ 44″ W

Date: Temp.:

Weather: ☀ ⛅ ☁ ❄ 🌧 💨
□ □ □ □ □ □

Season:

□ Spring □ Summer □ Fall □ Winter

Who I went with:

Lodging:

Fee(s):   □ Free:

Favorite moment:

Sights:

Wildlife:

Popular attractions:

□ Rouge Beach   □ Lake Audy Bison Enclosure
□ Bead Hill Historic Site   □ Bald Hill Trail
□ Mast Trail   □ Waterfront Bike Trail
□ Woodland Trail   □ The Trail
□ Orchard Trail   □ The WinterRouge Program
□ Celebration Forest Trail   □ Summer Learn-to-Camp Session
□ Tallgrass Trek   □ Glen Rouge Campground

of day(s) of visit

○ 1 ○ 2 ○ 3 ○ 3+

Overall Experience

10

Journal, Sketch, Photo & Passport Page

PHOTO & STAMP
HERE

Essential Gear

- ☐ This Book!
- ☐ Park Map
- ☐ Camera
- ☐ Sweater
- ☐ Binoculars
- ☐ Magnifying Glass
- ☐ Insect Repellent
- ☐ Water Bottle
- ☐ Snacks
- ☐ Swimsuit
- ☐ Towel
- ☐ First Aid Kit
- ☐ Hat
- ☐ Sunblock
- ☐ Pen/pencil
- ☐ Backpack
- ☐ Field Guide
- ☐ Trash Bag
- ☐ ----------
- ☐ ----------
- ☐ ----------
- ☐ ----------
- ☐ ----------
- ☐ ----------
- ☐ ----------

- ☐ ----------
- ☐ ----------
- ☐ ----------
- ☐ ----------
- ☐ ----------
- ☐ ----------
- ☐ ----------
- ☐ ----------
- ☐ ----------
- ☐ ----------
- ☐ ----------
- ☐ ----------
- ☐ ----------
- ☐ ----------
- ☐ ----------
- ☐ ----------
- ☐ ----------
- ☐ ----------
- ☐ ----------
- ☐ ----------
- ☐ ----------
- ☐ ----------
- ☐ ----------
- ☐ ----------
- ☐ ----------

- ☐ ----------
- ☐ ----------
- ☐ ----------
- ☐ ----------
- ☐ ----------
- ☐ ----------
- ☐ ----------
- ☐ ----------
- ☐ ----------
- ☐ ----------
- ☐ ----------
- ☐ ----------
- ☐ ----------
- ☐ ----------
- ☐ ----------
- ☐ ----------
- ☐ ----------
- ☐ ----------
- ☐ ----------
- ☐ ----------
- ☐ ----------
- ☐ ----------
- ☐ ----------
- ☐ ----------
- ☐ ----------

Sable Island

Nova Scotia | Est.: 2013 | Area (km²): 30 | Coord.: 43° 56′ 7″ N, 59° 54′ 25″ W

Date: Temp.:

Who I went with:

Weather: ☀ ⛅ 🌧 ❄ 🌦 💨
⬜ ⬜ ⬜ ⬜ ⬜ ⬜

Lodging:

Season:

⬜ Spring ⬜ Summer ⬜ Fall ⬜ Winter

Fee(s):   ⬜ Free:

Favorite moment:

Sights:

Wildlife:

Popular attractions:

⬜ The Bald Dune   ⬜ World Largest Grey Seal Colony
⬜ Wild Horses   ⬜ Historic Life-Saving Stations
⬜ ....   ⬜ ....
⬜ ....   ⬜ ....
⬜ ....   ⬜ ....
⬜ ....   ⬜ ....
⬜ ....   ⬜ ....

of day(s) of visit

⬜ 1 ⬜ 2 ⬜ 3 ⬜ 3+

Overall Experience

10

Journal, Sketch, Photo & Passport Page

PHOTO & STAMP HERE

Essential Gear

- [ ] This Book!
- [ ] Park Map
- [ ] Camera
- [ ] Sweater
- [ ] Binoculars
- [ ] Magnifying Glass
- [ ] Insect Repellent
- [ ] Water Bottle
- [ ] Snacks
- [ ] Swimsuit
- [ ] Towel
- [ ] First Aid Kit
- [ ] Hat
- [ ] Sunblock
- [ ] Pen/pencil
- [ ] Backpack
- [ ] Field Guide
- [ ] Trash Bag
- [ ] _____
- [ ] _____
- [ ] _____
- [ ] _____
- [ ] _____
- [ ] _____
- [ ] _____

- [ ] _____
- [ ] _____
- [ ] _____
- [ ] _____
- [ ] _____
- [ ] _____
- [ ] _____
- [ ] _____
- [ ] _____
- [ ] _____
- [ ] _____
- [ ] _____
- [ ] _____
- [ ] _____
- [ ] _____
- [ ] _____
- [ ] _____
- [ ] _____
- [ ] _____
- [ ] _____
- [ ] _____
- [ ] _____
- [ ] _____
- [ ] _____

- [ ] _____
- [ ] _____
- [ ] _____
- [ ] _____
- [ ] _____
- [ ] _____
- [ ] _____
- [ ] _____
- [ ] _____
- [ ] _____
- [ ] _____
- [ ] _____
- [ ] _____
- [ ] _____
- [ ] _____
- [ ] _____
- [ ] _____
- [ ] _____
- [ ] _____
- [ ] _____
- [ ] _____
- [ ] _____
- [ ] _____
- [ ] _____

Sirmilik

Nunavut | Est.: 2001 | Area (km²): 22,200 | Coord.: 72° 50′ 0″ N, 80° 35′ 0″ W

Date: Temp.:

Weather: ☀ ⛅ 🌧 ❄ 🌦 💨
⬜ ⬜ ⬜ ⬜ ⬜ ⬜

Season:

⬜ Spring ⬜ Summer ⬜ Fall ⬜ Winter

Who I went with:

Lodging:

Fee(s):   ⬜ Free:

Favorite moment:

Sights:

Wildlife:

Popular attractions:

⬜ Oliver Sound   ⬜ Bylot Island

⬜ Lancaster Sound   ⬜ Historic Life-Saving Stations

⬜ Navy Board Inlet   ⬜ Button Point Historical Sites

⬜ Eclipse Sound   ⬜ Baillarge Bay Sea Bird Colony

⬜ Mala River Valley   ⬜ World Largest Grey Seal Colony

⬜ Floe Edge Tours   ⬜ ....

⬜ Borden Peninsula   ⬜ ....

of day(s) of visit

◯ 1 ◯ 2 ◯ 3 ◯ 3+

Overall Experience

10

Journal, Sketch, Photo & Passport Page

PHOTO & STAMP
HERE

Essential Gear

- ☐ This Book!
- ☐ Park Map
- ☐ Camera
- ☐ Sweater
- ☐ Binoculars
- ☐ Magnifying Glass
- ☐ Insect Repellent
- ☐ Water Bottle
- ☐ Snacks
- ☐ Swimsuit
- ☐ Towel
- ☐ First Aid Kit
- ☐ Hat
- ☐ Sunblock
- ☐ Pen/pencil
- ☐ Backpack
- ☐ Field Guide
- ☐ Trash Bag
- ☐ -----------
- ☐ -----------
- ☐ -----------
- ☐ -----------
- ☐ -----------
- ☐ -----------
- ☐ -----------

- ☐ -----------
- ☐ -----------
- ☐ -----------
- ☐ -----------
- ☐ -----------
- ☐ -----------
- ☐ -----------
- ☐ -----------
- ☐ -----------
- ☐ -----------
- ☐ -----------
- ☐ -----------
- ☐ -----------
- ☐ -----------
- ☐ -----------
- ☐ -----------
- ☐ -----------
- ☐ -----------
- ☐ -----------
- ☐ -----------
- ☐ -----------
- ☐ -----------
- ☐ -----------
- ☐ -----------
- ☐ -----------

- ☐ -----------
- ☐ -----------
- ☐ -----------
- ☐ -----------
- ☐ -----------
- ☐ -----------
- ☐ -----------
- ☐ -----------
- ☐ -----------
- ☐ -----------
- ☐ -----------
- ☐ -----------
- ☐ -----------
- ☐ -----------
- ☐ -----------
- ☐ -----------
- ☐ -----------
- ☐ -----------
- ☐ -----------
- ☐ -----------
- ☐ -----------
- ☐ -----------
- ☐ -----------
- ☐ -----------
- ☐ -----------

Terra Nova

Newfoundland and Labrador | Est.: 1957 | Area (km²): 399 | Coord.: 48° 31′ 50″ N, 53° 55′ 41″ W

Date: Temp.:

Weather: ☼ ⛅ 🌧 ❄ 🌦 💨
⬜ ⬜ ⬜ ⬜ ⬜ ⬜

Who I went with:

Lodging:

Season:

⬜ Spring ⬜ Summer ⬜ Fall ⬜ Winter

Fee(s):   ⬜ Free:

Favorite moment:

Sights:

Wildlife:

Popular attractions:

⬜ Sandy Pond
⬜ Dunphy's Pond
⬜ Dunphy's Island
⬜ Malady Head Trail
⬜ The Visitor Centre
⬜ Blue Hill Lookout
⬜ Louil Hill Trail

⬜ Newman Sound
⬜ The Campfire Concert
⬜ Southwest Arm Trail
⬜ Heritage Trail
⬜ Kayaking the Atlantic Ocean
⬜ Ochre Hill Fire Tower
⬜ The Sea to Summit Hike

of day(s) of visit

⬭1 ⬭2 ⬭3 ⬭3+

Overall Experience

10

Journal, Sketch, Photo & Passport Page

PHOTO & STAMP HERE

Essential Gear

- [ ] This Book!
- [ ] Park Map
- [ ] Camera
- [ ] Sweater
- [ ] Binoculars
- [ ] Magnifying Glass
- [ ] Insect Repellent
- [ ] Water Bottle
- [ ] Snacks
- [ ] Swimsuit
- [ ] Towel
- [ ] First Aid Kit
- [ ] Hat
- [ ] Sunblock
- [ ] Pen/pencil
- [ ] Backpack
- [ ] Field Guide
- [ ] Trash Bag
- [ ] ----------
- [ ] ----------
- [ ] ----------
- [ ] ----------
- [ ] ----------
- [ ] ----------
- [ ] ----------

- [ ] ----------
- [ ] ----------
- [ ] ----------
- [ ] ----------
- [ ] ----------
- [ ] ----------
- [ ] ----------
- [ ] ----------
- [ ] ----------
- [ ] ----------
- [ ] ----------
- [ ] ----------
- [ ] ----------
- [ ] ----------
- [ ] ----------
- [ ] ----------
- [ ] ----------
- [ ] ----------
- [ ] ----------
- [ ] ----------
- [ ] ----------
- [ ] ----------
- [ ] ----------
- [ ] ----------
- [ ] ----------

- [ ] ----------
- [ ] ----------
- [ ] ----------
- [ ] ----------
- [ ] ----------
- [ ] ----------
- [ ] ----------
- [ ] ----------
- [ ] ----------
- [ ] ----------
- [ ] ----------
- [ ] ----------
- [ ] ----------
- [ ] ----------
- [ ] ----------
- [ ] ----------
- [ ] ----------
- [ ] ----------
- [ ] ----------
- [ ] ----------
- [ ] ----------
- [ ] ----------
- [ ] ----------
- [ ] ----------
- [ ] ----------

Thaidene Nëné

Northwest Territories | Est.: 2019 | Area (km²): 14,305 | Coord.: 62° 30′ 0″ N, 111° 0′ 0″ W

Date: **Temp.:** **Who I went with:**

Weather: ☀️ ⛅ ☁️ ❄️ 🌧️ 💨
☐ ☐ ☐ ☐ ☐ ☐

Lodging:

Season:

☐ Spring ☐ Summer ☐ Fall ☐ Winter

Fee(s): ☐ **Free:**

Favorite moment:

Sights:

Wildlife:

Popular attractions:

☐ Fort Reliance
☐ Great Slave Lake
☐ Tyrell Falls
☐ Our Lady of the Falls
☐ Lockhart River
☐ The Gap
☐ Wildbread Bay

☐ Kaché Abandoned Village Site
☐ Utsingi Point
☐ Artillery Lake
☐ Christie Bay
☐ The Barrenlands
☐ Berry Picking
☐ Northern Lights

# of day(s) of visit

☐ 1 ☐ 2 ☐ 3 ☐ 3+

Overall Experience

——
10

Journal, Sketch, Photo & Passport Page

PHOTO & STAMP
HERE

Essential Gear

- ☐ This Book!
- ☐ Park Map
- ☐ Camera
- ☐ Sweater
- ☐ Binoculars
- ☐ Magnifying Glass
- ☐ Insect Repellent
- ☐ Water Bottle
- ☐ Snacks
- ☐ Swimsuit
- ☐ Towel
- ☐ First Aid Kit
- ☐ Hat
- ☐ Sunblock
- ☐ Pen/pencil
- ☐ Backpack
- ☐ Field Guide
- ☐ Trash Bag
- ☐ ----------
- ☐ ----------
- ☐ ----------
- ☐ ----------
- ☐ ----------
- ☐ ----------
- ☐ ----------

Thousand Islands

Ontario | Est.: 1904 | Area (km²): 24.4 | Coord.: 44° 21′ 9″ N, 75° 57′ 18″ W

Date: Temp.:

Weather: ☀ ⛅ ☁ ❄ 🌧 💨
☐ ☐ ☐ ☐ ☐ ☐

Season:
☐ Spring ☐ Summer ☐ Fall ☐ Winter

Who I went with:

Lodging:

Fee(s):   ☐ Free:

Favorite moment:

Sights:

Wildlife:

Popular attractions:

☐ Gananoque Town   ☐ Mallorytown Landing
☐ Landon Bay   ☐ The Smoky Fire Trail
☐ The Lookout Trail   ☐ Six Nations Trail
☐ Garden Trail   ☐ Jones Creek
☐ Guided Therapy Walks ☐ Eel Loop
☐ Mallorytown Landing   ☐ Turtle Loop
☐ St. Lawrence River   ☐ Thousand Islands Parkway

of day(s) of visit

○ 1 ○ 2 ○ 3 ○ 3+

Overall Experience

10

Journal, Sketch, Photo & Passport Page

PHOTO & STAMP HERE

Essential Gear

- [ ] This Book!
- [ ] Park Map
- [ ] Camera
- [ ] Sweater
- [ ] Binoculars
- [ ] Magnifying Glass
- [ ] Insect Repellent
- [ ] Water Bottle
- [ ] Snacks
- [ ] Swimsuit
- [ ] Towel
- [ ] First Aid Kit
- [ ] Hat
- [ ] Sunblock
- [ ] Pen/pencil
- [ ] Backpack
- [ ] Field Guide
- [ ] Trash Bag
- [ ] _____
- [ ] _____
- [ ] _____
- [ ] _____
- [ ] _____
- [ ] _____
- [ ] _____

- [ ] _____
- [ ] _____
- [ ] _____
- [ ] _____
- [ ] _____
- [ ] _____
- [ ] _____
- [ ] _____
- [ ] _____
- [ ] _____
- [ ] _____
- [ ] _____
- [ ] _____
- [ ] _____
- [ ] _____
- [ ] _____
- [ ] _____
- [ ] _____
- [ ] _____
- [ ] _____
- [ ] _____
- [ ] _____
- [ ] _____
- [ ] _____
- [ ] _____

- [ ] _____
- [ ] _____
- [ ] _____
- [ ] _____
- [ ] _____
- [ ] _____
- [ ] _____
- [ ] _____
- [ ] _____
- [ ] _____
- [ ] _____
- [ ] _____
- [ ] _____
- [ ] _____
- [ ] _____
- [ ] _____
- [ ] _____
- [ ] _____
- [ ] _____
- [ ] _____
- [ ] _____
- [ ] _____
- [ ] _____
- [ ] _____
- [ ] _____

Torngat Mountains

Newfoundland and Labrador | Est.: 2008 | Area (km²): 9,700 | Coord.: 59° 26′ 9″ N, 63° 41′ 47″ W

Date: Temp.:   Who I went with:

Weather: ☀ ⛅ ☁ ❄ 🌧 💨
         ⬜ ⬜ ⬜ ⬜ ⬜ ⬜   Lodging:

Season:

⬜ Spring ⬜ Summer ⬜ Fall ⬜ Winter   Fee(s):   ⬜ Free:

Favorite moment:

Sights:

Wildlife:

Popular attractions:

⬜ Skull Lake   ⬜ Eclipse Channel
⬜ Emerald Lakes Area   ⬜ The North Arm (Silluak)
⬜ Iberville Valley   ⬜ Nakvak Brook
⬜ Palmer River Valley   ⬜ Nakvak Waterfalls
⬜ Rose Island   ⬜ Ramah Chert Quarries
⬜ The Inuksuk   ⬜ The Northern Lights
⬜ Old Village in Ramah   ⬜ Thousand Islands Parkway

# of day(s) of visit

◯1 ◯2 ◯3 ◯3+

Overall Experience

10

122

Journal, Sketch, Photo & Passport Page

PHOTO & STAMP
HERE

Essential Gear

- ☐ This Book!
- ☐ Park Map
- ☐ Camera
- ☐ Sweater
- ☐ Binoculars
- ☐ Magnifying Glass
- ☐ Insect Repellent
- ☐ Water Bottle
- ☐ Snacks
- ☐ Swimsuit
- ☐ Towel
- ☐ First Aid Kit
- ☐ Hat
- ☐ Sunblock
- ☐ Pen/pencil
- ☐ Backpack
- ☐ Field Guide
- ☐ Trash Bag
- ☐ ----------
- ☐ ----------
- ☐ ----------
- ☐ ----------
- ☐ ----------
- ☐ ----------
- ☐ ----------

- ☐ ----------
- ☐ ----------
- ☐ ----------
- ☐ ----------
- ☐ ----------
- ☐ ----------
- ☐ ----------
- ☐ ----------
- ☐ ----------
- ☐ ----------
- ☐ ----------
- ☐ ----------
- ☐ ----------
- ☐ ----------
- ☐ ----------
- ☐ ----------
- ☐ ----------
- ☐ ----------
- ☐ ----------
- ☐ ----------
- ☐ ----------
- ☐ ----------
- ☐ ----------
- ☐ ----------
- ☐ ----------

- ☐ ----------
- ☐ ----------
- ☐ ----------
- ☐ ----------
- ☐ ----------
- ☐ ----------
- ☐ ----------
- ☐ ----------
- ☐ ----------
- ☐ ----------
- ☐ ----------
- ☐ ----------
- ☐ ----------
- ☐ ----------
- ☐ ----------
- ☐ ----------
- ☐ ----------
- ☐ ----------
- ☐ ----------
- ☐ ----------
- ☐ ----------
- ☐ ----------
- ☐ ----------
- ☐ ----------
- ☐ ----------

Tuktut Nogait

Northwest Territories | Est.: 1998 | Area (km²): 18,890 | Coord.: 68° 49′ 07″ N, 121° 44′ 57″ W

Date: Temp.:

Weather: ☀️ ⛅ ☁️ ❄️ 🌧️ 💨
◻ ◻ ◻ ◻ ◻ ◻

Season:

◻ Spring   ◻ Summer   ◻ Fall   ◻ Winter

Who I went with:

Lodging:

Fee(s):   ◻ Free:

Favorite moment:

Sights:

Wildlife:

Popular attractions:

◻ Roscoe River   ◻ Brock Canyon

◻ Hornaday River   ◻ ....

◻ Hornaday River's Canyons   ◻ ....

◻ La Roncière Falls   ◻ ....

◻ Bluenose West Caribous   ◻ ....

◻ One Island Lake   ◻ ....

◻ Archaeological Sites   ◻ ....

of day(s) of visit

◯ 1   ◯ 2   ◯ 3   ◯ 3+

Overall Experience

10

Journal, Sketch, Photo & Passport Page

PHOTO & STAMP HERE

Essential Gear

- ☐ This Book!
- ☐ Park Map
- ☐ Camera
- ☐ Sweater
- ☐ Binoculars
- ☐ Magnifying Glass
- ☐ Insect Repellent
- ☐ Water Bottle
- ☐ Snacks
- ☐ Swimsuit
- ☐ Towel
- ☐ First Aid Kit
- ☐ Hat
- ☐ Sunblock
- ☐ Pen/pencil
- ☐ Backpack
- ☐ Field Guide
- ☐ Trash Bag
- ☐ ----------
- ☐ ----------
- ☐ ----------
- ☐ ----------
- ☐ ----------
- ☐ ----------
- ☐ ----------

- ☐ ----------
- ☐ ----------
- ☐ ----------
- ☐ ----------
- ☐ ----------
- ☐ ----------
- ☐ ----------
- ☐ ----------
- ☐ ----------
- ☐ ----------
- ☐ ----------
- ☐ ----------
- ☐ ----------
- ☐ ----------
- ☐ ----------
- ☐ ----------
- ☐ ----------
- ☐ ----------
- ☐ ----------
- ☐ ----------
- ☐ ----------
- ☐ ----------
- ☐ ----------
- ☐ ----------
- ☐ ----------

- ☐ ----------
- ☐ ----------
- ☐ ----------
- ☐ ----------
- ☐ ----------
- ☐ ----------
- ☐ ----------
- ☐ ----------
- ☐ ----------
- ☐ ----------
- ☐ ----------
- ☐ ----------
- ☐ ----------
- ☐ ----------
- ☐ ----------
- ☐ ----------
- ☐ ----------
- ☐ ----------
- ☐ ----------
- ☐ ----------
- ☐ ----------
- ☐ ----------
- ☐ ----------
- ☐ ----------
- ☐ ----------

Ukkusiksalik

Nunavut | Est.: 2003 | Area (km²): 20,885 | Coord.: 65° 29′ 55″ N, 88° 53′ 43″ W

Date: Temp.:

Who I went with:

Weather: ☼ ⛅ ☁ ❄ 🌧 💨
☐ ☐ ☐ ☐ ☐ ☐

Lodging:

Season:

☐ Spring ☐ Summer ☐ Fall ☐ Winter

Fee(s):   ☐ Free:

Favorite moment:

Sights:

Wildlife:

Popular attractions:

☐ Wager Bay   ☐ Aurora Borealis
☐ Sila River   ☐ ....
☐ Sila Lodge   ☐ ....
☐ Hudson's Bay Company   ☐ ....
☐ Aurora Borealis   ☐ ....
☐ Aklungiqtarvik   ☐ ....
☐ 500+ Archaeological Sites ☐ ....

# of day(s) of visit

○1 ○2 ○3 ○3+

Overall Experience

_____
10

128

Journal, Sketch, Photo & Passport Page

PHOTO & STAMP
HERE

Essential Gear

- [ ] This Book!
- [ ] Park Map
- [ ] Camera
- [ ] Sweater
- [ ] Binoculars
- [ ] Magnifying Glass
- [ ] Insect Repellent
- [ ] Water Bottle
- [ ] Snacks
- [ ] Swimsuit
- [ ] Towel
- [ ] First Aid Kit
- [ ] Hat
- [ ] Sunblock
- [ ] Pen/pencil
- [ ] Backpack
- [ ] Field Guide
- [ ] Trash Bag
- [ ] ----------
- [ ] ----------
- [ ] ----------
- [ ] ----------
- [ ] ----------
- [ ] ----------
- [ ] ----------

- [ ] ----------
- [ ] ----------
- [ ] ----------
- [ ] ----------
- [ ] ----------
- [ ] ----------
- [ ] ----------
- [ ] ----------
- [ ] ----------
- [ ] ----------
- [ ] ----------
- [ ] ----------
- [ ] ----------
- [ ] ----------
- [ ] ----------
- [ ] ----------
- [ ] ----------
- [ ] ----------
- [ ] ----------
- [ ] ----------
- [ ] ----------
- [ ] ----------
- [ ] ----------
- [ ] ----------
- [ ] ----------

- [ ] ----------
- [ ] ----------
- [ ] ----------
- [ ] ----------
- [ ] ----------
- [ ] ----------
- [ ] ----------
- [ ] ----------
- [ ] ----------
- [ ] ----------
- [ ] ----------
- [ ] ----------
- [ ] ----------
- [ ] ----------
- [ ] ----------
- [ ] ----------
- [ ] ----------
- [ ] ----------
- [ ] ----------
- [ ] ----------
- [ ] ----------
- [ ] ----------
- [ ] ----------
- [ ] ----------
- [ ] ----------

Vuntut

Yukon | Est.: 1995 | Area (km²): 4,345 | Coord.: 68° 24′ 37″ N, 139° 47′ 29″ W

Date: Temp.:

Who I went with:

Weather: ☼ ⛅ ☁ ❄ 🌧 💨
⬜ ⬜ ⬜ ⬜ ⬜ ⬜

Lodging:

Season:

⬜ Spring ⬜ Summer ⬜ Fall ⬜ Winter

Fee(s):   ⬜ Free:

Favorite moment:

Sights:

Wildlife:

Popular attractions:

⬜ Old Crow River   ⬜ Porcupine Caribou Migration

⬜ Sila River   ⬜ ....

⬜ Sila Lodge   ⬜ ....

⬜ John Tizya Centre   ⬜ ....

⬜ Van Tat (Old Crow Flats) ⬜ ....

⬜ British Mountains   ⬜ ....

⬜ Historic Caribou Fences ⬜ ....

# of day(s) of visit

◯1 ◯2 ◯3 ◯3+

Overall Experience

10

Journal, Sketch, Photo & Passport Page

PHOTO & STAMP HERE

Essential Gear

- [ ] This Book!
- [ ] Park Map
- [ ] Camera
- [ ] Sweater
- [ ] Binoculars
- [ ] Magnifying Glass
- [ ] Insect Repellent
- [ ] Water Bottle
- [ ] Snacks
- [ ] Swimsuit
- [ ] Towel
- [ ] First Aid Kit
- [ ] Hat
- [ ] Sunblock
- [ ] Pen/pencil
- [ ] Backpack
- [ ] Field Guide
- [ ] Trash Bag
- [ ] _____
- [ ] _____
- [ ] _____
- [ ] _____
- [ ] _____
- [ ] _____
- [ ] _____

Wapusk

Manitoba |Est.: 1996 | Area (km²): 11,475 | Coord.: 57° 46′ 26″ N, 93° 22′ 17″ W

Date: Temp.:

Who I went with:

Weather: ☀ ⛅ ☁ ❄ 🌧 🌬
☐ ☐ ☐ ☐ ☐ ☐

Lodging:

Season:

☐ Spring ☐ Summer ☐ Fall ☐ Winter

Fee(s):   ☐ Free:

Favorite moment:

Sights:

Wildlife:

Popular attractions:

☐ Polar Bear Viewing   ☐ The Heritage Railway Station
☐ Owl River   ☐ Tundra Buggy Lodge
☐ Owl River Camp   ☐ Northern Lights
☐ Broad River Camp   ☐ ....
☐ Cape Churchill   ☐ ....
☐ Snow Goose Hunt   ☐ ....
☐ Churchill Visitor Centre   ☐ ....

of day(s) of visit

○1 ○2 ○3 ○3+

Overall Experience

10

Journal, Sketch, Photo & Passport Page

PHOTO & STAMP HERE

Essential Gear

- [ ] This Book!
- [ ] Park Map
- [ ] Camera
- [ ] Sweater
- [ ] Binoculars
- [ ] Magnifying Glass
- [ ] Insect Repellent
- [ ] Water Bottle
- [ ] Snacks
- [ ] Swimsuit
- [ ] Towel
- [ ] First Aid Kit
- [ ] Hat
- [ ] Sunblock
- [ ] Pen/pencil
- [ ] Backpack
- [ ] Field Guide
- [ ] Trash Bag
- [ ] ----------
- [ ] ----------
- [ ] ----------
- [ ] ----------
- [ ] ----------
- [ ] ----------
- [ ] ----------

- [ ] ----------
- [ ] ----------
- [ ] ----------
- [ ] ----------
- [ ] ----------
- [ ] ----------
- [ ] ----------
- [ ] ----------
- [ ] ----------
- [ ] ----------
- [ ] ----------
- [ ] ----------
- [ ] ----------
- [ ] ----------
- [ ] ----------
- [ ] ----------
- [ ] ----------
- [ ] ----------
- [ ] ----------
- [ ] ----------
- [ ] ----------
- [ ] ----------
- [ ] ----------

- [ ] ----------
- [ ] ----------
- [ ] ----------
- [ ] ----------
- [ ] ----------
- [ ] ----------
- [ ] ----------
- [ ] ----------
- [ ] ----------
- [ ] ----------
- [ ] ----------
- [ ] ----------
- [ ] ----------
- [ ] ----------
- [ ] ----------
- [ ] ----------
- [ ] ----------
- [ ] ----------
- [ ] ----------
- [ ] ----------
- [ ] ----------
- [ ] ----------
- [ ] ----------

Waterton Lakes

Alberta |Est.: 1895 | Area (km²): 505 | Coord.: 49° 5' 40" N, 113° 51' 42" W

Date: Temp.:

Weather: ☀ ⛅ 🌧 ❄ 🌦 💨
⬭ ⬭ ⬭ ⬭ ⬭ ⬭

Who I went with:

Lodging:

Season:

⬭ Spring   ⬭ Summer   ⬭ Fall   ⬭ Winter

Fee(s):   ⬭ Free:

Favorite moment:

Sights:

Wildlife:

Popular attractions:

⬭ The Entrance Parkway   ⬭ Cameron Lakeshore Trail

⬭ Red Rock Parkway   ⬭ Bear's Hump Trail

⬭ Kootenai Brown Trail   ⬭ The Maskinonge

⬭ Chief Mountain Highway   ⬭ Waterton Lakes Golf Course

⬭ Bison Paddock Overlook   ⬭ Bar U Ranch Historic Site

⬭ Bertha Falls   ⬭ Prince of Wales Hotel

⬭ Blakiston Falls Trail   ⬭ International Peace Park Plaza

of day(s) of visit

◯1   ◯2   ◯3   ◯3+

Overall Experience

10

Journal, Sketch, Photo & Passport Page

PHOTO & STAMP HERE

Essential Gear

- ☐ This Book!
- ☐ Park Map
- ☐ Camera
- ☐ Sweater
- ☐ Binoculars
- ☐ Magnifying Glass
- ☐ Insect Repellent
- ☐ Water Bottle
- ☐ Snacks
- ☐ Swimsuit
- ☐ Towel
- ☐ First Aid Kit
- ☐ Hat
- ☐ Sunblock
- ☐ Pen/pencil
- ☐ Backpack
- ☐ Field Guide
- ☐ Trash Bag
- ☐ -----------
- ☐ -----------
- ☐ -----------
- ☐ -----------
- ☐ -----------
- ☐ -----------
- ☐ -----------

- ☐ -----------
- ☐ -----------
- ☐ -----------
- ☐ -----------
- ☐ -----------
- ☐ -----------
- ☐ -----------
- ☐ -----------
- ☐ -----------
- ☐ -----------
- ☐ -----------
- ☐ -----------
- ☐ -----------
- ☐ -----------
- ☐ -----------
- ☐ -----------
- ☐ -----------
- ☐ -----------
- ☐ -----------
- ☐ -----------
- ☐ -----------
- ☐ -----------
- ☐ -----------
- ☐ -----------
- ☐ -----------

- ☐ -----------
- ☐ -----------
- ☐ -----------
- ☐ -----------
- ☐ -----------
- ☐ -----------
- ☐ -----------
- ☐ -----------
- ☐ -----------
- ☐ -----------
- ☐ -----------
- ☐ -----------
- ☐ -----------
- ☐ -----------
- ☐ -----------
- ☐ -----------
- ☐ -----------
- ☐ -----------
- ☐ -----------
- ☐ -----------
- ☐ -----------
- ☐ -----------
- ☐ -----------
- ☐ -----------
- ☐ -----------

Wood Buffalo

Alberta and N. T. |Est.: 1922 | Area (km²): 44,807 | Coord.: 60° 16′ 0″ N, 114° 10′ 4″ W

Date: Temp.:   Who I went with:

Weather: ☀ ⛅ 🌧 ❄ 🌦 💨
         ☐ ☐ ☐ ☐ ☐ ☐   Lodging:

Season:

☐ Spring ☐ Summer ☐ Fall ☐ Winter   Fee(s):   ☐ Free:

Favorite moment:

Sights:

Wildlife:

Popular attractions: # of day(s) of visit

☐ Salt Plains Lookout   ☐ Salt River Meadows Trail   ☐ 1 ☐ 2 ☐ 3 ☐ 3+
☐ The Sky Circle   ☐ World's Largest Beaver Dam
☐ Nyarling River Pull-Off ☐ F. Chipewyan Reception Centre   **Overall**
☐ Benchmark Creek Trail   ☐ Sweetgrass Station B.C. Camp   **Experience**
☐ Peace-Athabasca Delta   ☐ Pine Lake
☐ Angus Sinkhole   ☐ Pine Lake Campground   ____
☐ Karstland Trail   ☐ Weekly Campfire Program   **10**

Journal, Sketch, Photo & Passport Page

PHOTO & STAMP HERE

Essential Gear

- [ ] This Book!
- [ ] Park Map
- [ ] Camera
- [ ] Sweater
- [ ] Binoculars
- [ ] Magnifying Glass
- [ ] Insect Repellent
- [ ] Water Bottle
- [ ] Snacks
- [ ] Swimsuit
- [ ] Towel
- [ ] First Aid Kit
- [ ] Hat
- [ ] Sunblock
- [ ] Pen/pencil
- [ ] Backpack
- [ ] Field Guide
- [ ] Trash Bag
- [ ] ----------
- [ ] ----------
- [ ] ----------
- [ ] ----------
- [ ] ----------
- [ ] ----------
- [ ] ----------

- [ ] ----------
- [ ] ----------
- [ ] ----------
- [ ] ----------
- [ ] ----------
- [ ] ----------
- [ ] ----------
- [ ] ----------
- [ ] ----------
- [ ] ----------
- [ ] ----------
- [ ] ----------
- [ ] ----------
- [ ] ----------
- [ ] ----------
- [ ] ----------
- [ ] ----------
- [ ] ----------
- [ ] ----------
- [ ] ----------
- [ ] ----------
- [ ] ----------
- [ ] ----------
- [ ] ----------
- [ ] ----------

- [ ] ----------
- [ ] ----------
- [ ] ----------
- [ ] ----------
- [ ] ----------
- [ ] ----------
- [ ] ----------
- [ ] ----------
- [ ] ----------
- [ ] ----------
- [ ] ----------
- [ ] ----------
- [ ] ----------
- [ ] ----------
- [ ] ----------
- [ ] ----------
- [ ] ----------
- [ ] ----------
- [ ] ----------
- [ ] ----------
- [ ] ----------
- [ ] ----------
- [ ] ----------
- [ ] ----------
- [ ] ----------

Yoho

British Columbia |Est.: 1922 | Area (km²): 1,313 | Coord.: 51° 30′ 0″ N, 116° 30′ 0″ W

Date: Temp.: | Who I went with:

Weather: ☀ ⛅ ☁ ❄ 🌧 🌬 |
⬜ ⬜ ⬜ ⬜ ⬜ ⬜ | Lodging:

Season:

⬜ Spring ⬜ Summer ⬜ Fall ⬜ Winter | Fee(s):   ⬜ Free:

Favorite moment:

Sights:

Wildlife:

Popular attractions:

		# of day(s) of visit
⬜ Takakkaw Falls	⬜ Iceline Trail	◯1 ◯2 ◯3 ◯3+
⬜ Burgess Shale Fossils	⬜ Laughing Falls	
⬜ Emerald Lake	⬜ Paget Lookout	**Overall**
⬜ The Natural Bridge	⬜ Great Divide Trail	**Experience**
⬜ Lake O'Hara	⬜ Field Village	
⬜ Wapta Falls	⬜ Walk-in-the-Past Trail	
⬜ Spiral Tunnels Lookout	⬜ Ross Lake Trail	**10**

Journal, Sketch, Photo & Passport Page

PHOTO & STAMP
HERE

Essential Gear

- ☐ This Book!
- ☐ Park Map
- ☐ Camera
- ☐ Sweater
- ☐ Binoculars
- ☐ Magnifying Glass
- ☐ Insect Repellent
- ☐ Water Bottle
- ☐ Snacks
- ☐ Swimsuit
- ☐ Towel
- ☐ First Aid Kit
- ☐ Hat
- ☐ Sunblock
- ☐ Pen/pencil
- ☐ Backpack
- ☐ Field Guide
- ☐ Trash Bag
- ☐ ----------
- ☐ ----------
- ☐ ----------
- ☐ ----------
- ☐ ----------
- ☐ ----------
- ☐ ----------

- ☐ ----------
- ☐ ----------
- ☐ ----------
- ☐ ----------
- ☐ ----------
- ☐ ----------
- ☐ ----------
- ☐ ----------
- ☐ ----------
- ☐ ----------
- ☐ ----------
- ☐ ----------
- ☐ ----------
- ☐ ----------
- ☐ ----------
- ☐ ----------
- ☐ ----------
- ☐ ----------
- ☐ ----------
- ☐ ----------
- ☐ ----------
- ☐ ----------
- ☐ ----------
- ☐ ----------
- ☐ ----------

- ☐ ----------
- ☐ ----------
- ☐ ----------
- ☐ ----------
- ☐ ----------
- ☐ ----------
- ☐ ----------
- ☐ ----------
- ☐ ----------
- ☐ ----------
- ☐ ----------
- ☐ ----------
- ☐ ----------
- ☐ ----------
- ☐ ----------
- ☐ ----------
- ☐ ----------
- ☐ ----------
- ☐ ----------
- ☐ ----------
- ☐ ----------
- ☐ ----------
- ☐ ----------
- ☐ ----------
- ☐ ----------

| | Est.: | Area (km²): | Coord.: |

Date: Temp.:   Who I went with:

Weather: ☀ ⛅ 🌧 ❄ 🌦 🌬
         ☐ ☐ ☐ ☐ ☐ ☐   Lodging:

Season:

☐ Spring ☐ Summer ☐ Fall ☐ Winter   Fee(s):   ☐ Free:

Favorite moment:

Sights:

Wildlife:

Popular attractions: **# of day(s) of visit**

☐ .... ☐ ....   ○1 ○2 ○3 ○3+
☐ .... ☐ ....
☐ .... ☐ ....   **Overall**
☐ .... ☐ ....   **Experience**
☐ .... ☐ ....
☐ .... ☐ ....   —
☐ .... ☐   10

Journal, Sketch, Photo & Passport Page

PHOTO & STAMP HERE

Essential Gear

- [ ] This Book!
- [ ] Park Map
- [ ] Camera
- [ ] Sweater
- [ ] Binoculars
- [ ] Magnifying Glass
- [ ] Insect Repellent
- [ ] Water Bottle
- [ ] Snacks
- [ ] Swimsuit
- [ ] Towel
- [ ] First Aid Kit
- [ ] Hat
- [ ] Sunblock
- [ ] Pen/pencil
- [ ] Backpack
- [ ] Field Guide
- [ ] Trash Bag
- [ ] ----------
- [ ] ----------
- [ ] ----------
- [ ] ----------
- [ ] ----------
- [ ] ----------
- [ ] ----------

|Est.: | Area (km²): | Coord.:

Date: Temp.:

Weather: ☀ ⛅ ☁ ❄ 🌧 🌬
         ⬭ ⬭ ⬭ ⬭ ⬭ ⬭

Who I went with:

Lodging:

Season:

⬭ Spring ⬭ Summer ⬭ Fall ⬭ Winter

Fee(s):   ⬭ Free:

Favorite moment:

Sights:

Wildlife:

Popular attractions:

⬭ .... ⬭ ....
⬭ .... ⬭ ....
⬭ .... ⬭ ....
⬭ .... ⬭ ....
⬭ .... ⬭ ....
⬭ .... ⬭ ....
⬭ .... ⬭ ....

# of day(s) of visit
⬭1 ⬭2 ⬭3 ⬭3+

**Overall
Experience**

——
10

Journal, Sketch, Photo & Passport Page

PHOTO & STAMP HERE